# UNMASKING THE HACKER

*Demystifying cybercrime*

## AMANDA-JANE TURNER

© Copyright Amanda-Jane Turner 2019

All rights reserved. Except as permitted under the Australian Copyright Act 1968 (for example, a fair dealing for the purposes of study, research, criticism or review), no part of this book may be reproduced, stored in a retrieval system, communicated or transmitted in any form or by any means without prior written permission. All enquiries should be made to the author.

*This book is dedicated to my husband, **Andrew Clarke**, who is the best human I know. He patiently tempers my eccentricity with common sense and puts up with, and encourages, my many eclectic interests, need for coffee, chocolate, art supplies, technology, game consoles, books and, many pets.*

# FOREWORD

Cybercrime is a confronting topic for most. Technology engineered to improve our lives has become a vector for criminals to exploit us. Internet connected devices have opened our personal lives to the world, unexpectedly bringing additional and often misunderstood considerations for our personal security.

Even more confronting is the hype generated from advanced malware, some tools previously used in warfighting by nation states, being used to exploit the average person. The picture of an individual wearing a black hoody sitting in a dark room is etched in our minds as the typical hacker. An unknown entity with access to military grade weapons that nobody can see or understand. Understandably, this image can invoke a feeling of despair to anyone without experience in cyber security.

Thankfully, there are many intelligent people in the cyber security industry pulling apart the technology and tactics used by these criminals, combined with individuals in complementary industries such as banking and finance pulling apart money laundering rings to prevent criminals from receiving the proceeds of crime.

One such person is Amanda Jane Turner. Her dedication to tackling these threats head on and educating the community from her experiences is commendable. I hope this edition imparts a portion of her wisdom built up from 20 years in government and community participation to illuminate the seemingly shadowy world of cyber attacks.

..........................

*Cody Byrnes*
*Senior Cyber Security Analyst*

# ACKNOWLEDGMENTS

*This book came to a fruition because of the support of my husband as well as my infosec and academic peers.* Special thanks goes to my husband **Andrew Clarke** for always encouraging me, and to the following for their ongoing support: **Alex Kenley**, Director - Threat Vector Security, **Nicole Stephensen**, Principal Consultant - Ground Up Consulting; **Mike Holm** & **AusCERT**; My Team - **Kieran Chow**, **Marek Krawus**, **David Fairbrother** & **David Shrimpton; AISA** & **AWSN**; and **Cody Byrnes**, **Shelly Mills**, **Sasenka Abeysooriya**, **Pops Hartley**, **Jacqui Kernot**, **James Culverhous**e, **Kristine Sihto**, **Sarah Bennett**, **Lorraine Mazerolle**, **Jonah Rimer**, & **Cass Cross**.

Thanks also to all who support victims, or police cybercrime - helping to make our community safer; these include **Moises S (IDCare)**, **Scott B (QPS)** and **Marty A, Claire A** & **Tash V (AFP)**.

# INTRODUCTION

A realisation, that cybercrime and cyber security are often seen as mysterious to many users of technology, motivated me to start an initiative I call the Demystify Cyber project. This project which includes creating this book aims to help everyone to be safer online and when using technology.

Popular culture's portrayal of cybercrime as being perpetrated by hoody-wearing hackers is a stereotype that encourages a mystique around cybercrime. This stereotype contributes to the lack of cybercrime awareness in the community and may encourage cyber security appearing as an unattainable highly technical ideal. Concerned over the amount of people being impacted by cybercrime and wanting to banish harmful hacker stereotypes, I decided to write a book aimed at a largely non-technical audience to help demystify cybercrime and make cyber security familiar, understandable and accessible to all people. Just as we lock our doors when we leave the house to protect from burglars, the way we protect ourselves from cybercrime should be as easy. We need to stop the hoody-wearing elite hacker narrative and talk about how cybercrime is just another crime type that we do not have to be highly technical to protect ourselves from.

As technology has evolved exponentially since the advent of the Internet, and because each subsequent generation does not know a time without being connected via smart phones and emails, this book provides a brief history of computing and the Internet, hacking, social engineering and cybercrime. The book in its entirety endeavours to show the reader that scams using or against technology are not new and that they are crime that we can do things to protect ourselves against without the need for being highly computer literate. There is also discussion of some public domain cybercrime and hacker examples, a chapter on the challenges of policing cybercrime and, lastly the book shares how the non-technical and technical alike can increase their awareness of, and protection from cybercrime.

I have worked in the information security industry in a variety of roles, including fraud investigations and analysis, cybercrime intelligence and cybersecurity risk and incident response, for many years, spoken at conferences, lectured on cybercrime and cybersecurity and, mentored people new to the information security industry. The topic of cybercrime is something I am very interested in and, I believe it needs to be demystified so all people can understand it and protect themselves better. There is no solely technical solution to cyber security and neither is there solely a human solution, this is why anyone who uses computers, smartphones and the Internet need to have an understanding of what is in their power to do to protect themselves from crime against or enabled by technology.

There are many books in the market about cyber security and some very interesting academic reference books on cybercrime. This book seeks to complement these by providing an accessible narrative about cybercrime and cyber security. It is my hope that the book will be read by a larger audience both technical and non-technical and help raise awareness of cybercrime. Please read this book, discuss it with your friends and family, disagree and debate with me, and most importantly please help to get cybercrime awareness into the hands of everyone. As the world becomes more connected with technology, cyber security is increasingly becoming everybody's business.

There is a glossary of terms at the back of the book as even though this book aims to demystify cybercrime, some computer or malware terms are difficult to avoid!

This book is intended as a basic and brief overview of cybercrime and cyber security to support all users of technology to be safer in cyberspace.

# CONTENTS

**Part One**
**A BRIEF HISTORY OF CYBERCRIME**

1. The first hacker?   3
2. Golden age of hacking   8
3. End of the 20th Century and Y2K   16
4. Cybercrime in the 21st century   23

**Part Two**
**CYBERCRIME - SCAMS**

5. Phishing   33
6. Business email compromise   41
7. Tech support scams   49
8. Other cyber enabled scams   54

**Part Three**
**CYBERCRIME - MALWARE**

9. DDoS and botnets   69
10. Spyware, malvertising and logic bombs   78
11. Trojans, key loggers and cryptojacking   87
12. Ransomware   93

**Part Four**
**CYBERCRIME - THE PHYSICAL WORLD**

13. Cybercrime - bullying and exploitation   105
14. Data breaches and privacy   109
15. Cybercrime - the perpetrators   113
16. Cybercrime - challenges for law enforcement   117

**Part Five**
## CYBER SECURITY

| | |
|---|---|
| 17. What is cybersecurity? | 123 |
| 18. Technology for cybersecurity | 127 |
| 19. Cybersecurity - vulnerabilities | 131 |
| 20. Careers in cyber security | 135 |

**Part Six**
## DEMYSTIFY AND MITIGATE

| | |
|---|---|
| 21. A brief history of computers | 143 |
| 22. The world of the web | 148 |
| 23. Protection from cybercrime | 153 |
| 24. Unmasking the hacker | 164 |
| | |
| Where to go for help | 171 |
| Notes | 175 |
| Glossary | 187 |
| Index | 197 |
| About the Demystify Cyber project | 201 |
| | |
| About the Author | 203 |

*Part One*

# A BRIEF HISTORY OF CYBERCRIME

Part one of *Unmasking the Hacker* provides a brief summary of some of the more significant events in the history of computing, hacking and cybercrime. Using examples from history, the following chapters serve to demonstrate that people who commit cybercrime are far removed from the stereotypical hoody wearing hackers popularised in fiction. To demystify cybercrime, unmask the mysterious hacker and learn how to better protect ourselves from cybercrime, it helps to understand more about the history of computing, and different types of hacking and cybercrime campaigns.

Crime against or enabled by technology is older than some may realise, in fact it dates back to way before the Internet. Attacks against technology with sabotage of punch card controlled automated machinery, for example, occurred in the early 1800s. Hacking of long-distance communication signals is also not a modern crime, with a famous incident occurring in the

1900s. These crimes against or enabled by technology clearly predate modern computing. The following chapters look at historical examples of crime against or enabled by technology and provide a very brief overview of cybercrime, infamous hackers and phone phreaks with examples of the criminals and their campaigns between the years 1801 to 2019.

Chapter one looks at crime against or enabled by technology that occurred well before the advent of the Internet. There is also discussion of the person who very possibly is history's first hacker, a man who intercepted and inserted his own messages into allegedly secure private long-distance wireless telegraph signals. Chapter two provides a summary of the golden age of hacking as tinkering with, learning about and enhancing technology was the aim rather than crime. Chapter three provides a brief overview of the malicious cyber activities of the late twentieth century including an overview of some infamous hackers and, to contextualise the timeline, also briefly looks at the Y2K, or millennium, bug. The last chapter in this section gives a summary of some of the more significant cybercrime activities, such as DDoS attacks, viruses and other malware campaigns affecting the early twenty-first century.

This section looks at crime against technology that dates as far back as the nineteenth century, to show that sabotage of technology and security incidents like signal hacking are crimes that predate the Internet.

## Chapter One
# THE FIRST HACKER?

"There was a young fellow of Italy, who diddled the public quite prettily" – Maskelyne[1]

Throughout this book the term cybercrime is used to refer to any crime against or enabled by technology. This term also encompasses far more than hacking, malware or phishing. Cybercrime, using this definition, is much older than some may realise with security incidents impacting technology occurring well before the advent of desk top computers, the internet and smart phones. To demystify cybercrime, unmask the shadowy hacker of legend and, gain a better understanding of how all users of technology can enhance their own cybersecurity and protection from cybercrime, it is important to understand that this crime type is neither mystical nor modern. Historical records and research, for example, show that crime targeting computerised or automated devices dates all the way back to the early 1800s with the advent of the punch card automated loom in France. Similarly, hacking into private message transmissions and disrupting long-distance communication signals can be traced back to at least 1903.

In 1801, to put this into historical perspective, the year Thomas Jefferson was sworn in as the third President of the United States[2], and the French astronomer Jean-Louis Pons discovered a comet[3], another Frenchman, Joseph Jacquard, exhibited his new technological invention. Jacquard developed and created a type of programmable technology for weaving textile designs using a punch card that controlled and automated designs in his factory's looms[4]. Jacquard, a textile merchant, originally worked on designs for an automated loom in the 1790s, however his work was delayed due to the French Revolution. If it wasn't for the French revolution delaying his work on an automated loom, there may have been an even earlier instance of crime against technology! The Jacquard loom was an early computer and the chained together punch cards, that used a binary system to instruct the loom to automatically create the desired designs, influenced the work of computing pioneer Charles Babbage's Analytical Engine[5].

This punch card technology advanced textile manufacturing significantly and, by automating many loom functions, also threatened jobs. Prior to Jacquard's punch card automated loom, children were employed by the textile factories to manually raise threads to create the intricate designs in the woven fabric. Concern that this automated loom technology would leave children with no jobs to support their impoverished families, Jacquard's invention was often sabotaged by activists and disgruntled employees.[6] Although these events occurred in the nineteenth century and relate to physical crime against technology, they echo the concepts we know today in the twenty-first century, as hacktivism or even insider threats.

Going forward a century, and again to provide historical context, this was the year 1903 that saw suffragette Lady Dollan fight to secure the vote for women[7], the first ever Tour de France bicycle race was held[8] and, an Italian named Guglielmo Marconi shared with the world his trans-Atlantic wireless communication technology [9]. Marconi was proud of his newest invention and publicly claimed it provided secure and private long-distance messaging capability.

Not everyone was impressed by Marconi's work however, and in fact he had a rival in another creative peer, John Nevil Maskelyne. Maskelyne, an illusionist, inventor, and businessman performed on stage and used Morse code to communicate with his assistants to perform his mind reading tricks. Maskelyne also invented a variety of techniques to use in his performances, including devising a transmitter to remotely ignite gunpowder, however when attempting to patent some of his inventions he was often foiled by the patents that Marconi had already registered[10].

During a lecture at the Royal Institute, by the well-respected physicist and electrical engineer Ambrose Fleming, showcasing Marconi's much proclaimed secure and private long-distance communication technology, a security incident occurred which Maskelyne later accepted responsibility for. While Fleming was setting up the communications apparatus with the aim to receiving a secure message from Marconi, the device started to receive a message. The message in Morse code at first repeated the word 'rats', however once the perpetrator had their attention, the message then spelled out a limerick accusing the Italian inventor of defrauding the public. Maskelyne, happy to accept responsibility for intercepting the much-hyped secure and private radio signal, felt it was necessary to demonstrate that the communications device was not as secure as Marconi had advertised. While Marconi is considered a pioneer in long-distance radio transmissions, Maskelyne could well be the first hacker of purportedly secure and private transmissions.

These examples of crime against or enabled by technology occurred well before the development of modern computers or the Internet. With disgruntled employees and activists in the 1800s sabotaging the punch card automated looms to show dissatisfaction and fear at job losses and Maskelyne's intercept of radio waves in the 1900s to demonstrate that Marconi's long-distance communication technology was not secure, cybercrime existed as early as two centuries ago. Although it went by a different name and wasn't popularised by pictures of shadowy hackers in hoodies, cybercrime[11] predates modern computers, computing tablets, smart phones and the Internet. These historical examples of sabotage of technology and unauthorised signal intercepts, or hacked radio signals, were not called cybercrime at the time and the criminals perpetrating these crimes were not known as hackers, however these are early examples of crime against or enabled by technology.

## Key Takeaways

- Cybercrime is a term denoting any crime against or enabled by technology.
- Incidents of cybercrime date back to well before the Internet or modern computing.
- In the 1800s, Jacquard's punch card automated loom technology was sabotaged by disgruntled employees.
- In the 1900s, Marconi promoted his wireless communication invention as secure and private technology, however in 1903 Maskelyne hacked into the signal to prove that the technology was neither private nor secure.

## Chapter Two
# GOLDEN AGE OF HACKING

"Mr. Eccles requests that anyone working or hacking on the electrical system turn the power off to avoid fuse blowing" [1]

The golden age of hacking describes a simpler time, well before smart phones and portable computers. Hacking in the earlier days of modern computing was often done by students who were exploring what technology could do and devising ways to enhance it. A fascination for how the telephone network operated led to some learning how to exploit it to get free phone calls. The first ransomware campaign was sent by actual physical post and, code created allegedly to measure a computer network inadvertently turned into a worm! These people do not fit the stereotype of the malicious hacker popularised in modern day fiction, news and popular culture.

To help demystify hacking and show that the perpetrators of cybercrime are not all stereotypical masked or hooded criminal figures, it pays to establish where the term originated. It may be surprising to some that the term hacker does not derive from the activities of ominous hoody wearing criminals, but instead the term is thought to originate in the mid 1950s with a model railroad club. Students who were members of the Massachusetts Institute of Technology (MIT) Tech Model Railroad Club used the terms hacking and hackers to refer to tinkering with and enhancing technology. The club members discovered ways to modify the train signals and create complicated track designs [2] later turning their attention to modifying computer programming[3]. Historical records show meeting minutes from the group in 1955 where the members were requested to turn off the power, on the technology they were hacking, to prevent fuses blowing. This hacking is less about malicious interference of technology and more about experimentation.

Also in the 1950s, a young blind boy with perfect pitch, Josef Engressia Jr.[4], learned to mimic the operator tones, whistles and clicks of the telephone system. By the 1960s he was whistling into phones to obtain free long-distance calls, gaining him the nickname of the Whistler. He later changed his name to Joy Bubbles [5], and is known as one of the first phone phreaks. Phone phreaks, like the MIT Tech Model Railroad Club hackers, enjoyed learning about and exploring technology, specifically the telephone systems. They listened to and memorised the tones made while calls were being connected and read about telephones and how they worked. They also explored social engineering techniques to trick telephony employees into giving them information about how the telephone networks worked and the operator tones used. This curiosity in how telephones work led them to exploit the phone system by mimicking the connection tones to place free calls, which was a type of technology enabled fraud.

Following on from Engressia's early telephone exploration and exploitation, came John Draper, a pirate radio station enthusiast, who was asked by another phone phreak Denny Teresi[6], to create a tone generator known as a Blue Box. The Blue Box was a device that had a keypad, amplifier and speaker and it was used in generation of the tone needed to exploit vulnerabilities in the phone system to trick it into providing free calls. The blue boxes used by phone phreaks were thought to have been invented by an engineering student named, Ralph Barclay[7], who built a 2600hz tone generator in 1960. The first multi frequency box he created was in a blue box, which gave the name to future phone phreaking devices regardless of their colour. In 1972, two people now famous for creating Apple computers, Steve Wozniak and Steve Jobs[8]., also showed a strong interest in phone phreaking, and their hacking exploits were apparently done under the names under the names Berkley Blue and Oaf Tobar respectively. They built blue boxes for themselves and also sold them to other Berkley students[9]. While experimenting with frequencies to exploit the telephone networks, Draper discovered that a toy whistle given away in packets of cereal generated the exact pitch of 2600 Hz that was needed to access the operator mode of telephone calls. The cereal was called Captain Crunch, and John Draper was thereafter known by that moniker during his phone phreaking exploits. Draper's phone phreaking earned him two prison sentences in 1976 and 1978.

Another person interested in phone phreaking, was Kevin Mitnick, who later became infamous for his social engineering, hacking and subsequent arrests. Mitnick researched and learned enough about phone companies to use social engineering to trick phone company employees to providing him with the information he needed. Social engineering is a type of confidence trick or scam, where psychological manipulation is used to gain confidential information or unauthorised access to a restricted area or network. Armed with the insider information, Mitnick was able to make free long distance or trunk calls, access unlisted phone numbers and, at one point he had control of the Pacific Bell telephone network[10]. In 1979 while still a teenager Mitnick accessed the Ark, which was the restricted computer system of the Digital Equipment Corporation and copied the software. Mitnick used what is now known as social engineering to access the information. These techniques have success because they exploit human reactions or tendency to trust or to want to help. Armed with the name and contact number of the Ark's system administrator, Mitnick contacted him and pretended to be one of the developers. Claiming he couldn't log into his account, Mitnick persuaded the system administrator to provide him with new credentials and the dial-up password. Gaining the employee's trust, Mitnick was provided with all the information he needed to access the Ark, Mitnick is one of the world's most well-known hackers[11] and, despite popular concepts that hackers are shadowy figures dressed in hoodies that feverishly type code to hack into systems, Mitnick accessed the systems of many organisations, including forty large corporations, mainly by using social engineering techniques. As an aside, these days Mr Mitnick s a well-respected cyber security consultant, author[12] and conference speaker.

In 1983, under the alias Dark Dante, a teenager named Kevin Poulsen accessed the Internet's ancestor, ARPANET.[13] Unlike the modern Internet where a Uniform Resource Locator (URL) address is used to access a website, accessing networks via the ARPANET required specific phone numbers to be called. The teenaged Poulsen allegedly had found one of these phone numbers for a restricted network, and after connecting his modem and dialling in, he found himself in a database of restricted military research. It was only after he inadvertently used his real name while accessing the network, after three weeks of systematic undetected intrusion, that he was discovered, and his computer was confiscated. This did not stop Poulsen's foray into cybercrime however, in 1990 when a radio station offered a prize of a luxury car to a caller to the station Poulsen was instrumental in taking over the station's phone lines. Poulsen penetrated the computer networks of the radio station to control all its phone lines, in order to be the caller that won a Porsche. Kevin Poulsen later served prison time for wire fraud[14].

Five years later, ARPANET was again the target, when in the same vein that early hacking, phone phreaking and social engineering came about because of curiosity in technology, a denial of service (DoS) impacted the network. A DoS attack in basic terms, is when a huge amount of computer queries targets a network and tie up all the resources so no legitimate requests can be responded to. In November 1988 Robert Morris, a Cornell university graduate student, created and released code on to ARPANET from an MIT computer, allegedly to measure the size of the network. The code, although not necessarily meant as malware, had a spreading mechanism and was created to self-replicate. It spread rapidly through ARPANET and impacted around 10% of the 60,000 computing devices on the network.[15] This code become known as the malware, the Morris Worm, and Robert Morris was the first person convicted under the USA's 1986 Computer Fraud and Abuse Act.

In addition to this early form of DoS malware, the eighties also saw the first instance of Ransomware. Ransomware is a type of cybercrime where malware is used to lock down or encrypt a computer's files or limit a user's access to the computer until a ransom has been paid. In 1989, during the height of the AIDS epidemic[16], Dr. Joseph Popp, a biologist, sent 20,000 floppy disks to other researchers in the world on the pretext that they contained software to determine a patient's risk of becoming infected with the AIDS virus. Although the disks did contain a type of AIDS risk assessment application, they also contained malware. The malware started after a computer had been rebooted ninety times[17], and locked down access to the computer. The computer user was then presented with a ransom message on the screen and instructed the computer's user to turn on the printer.

The ransom note was then printed with instructions for the user to pay for a software lease and send it to an address in Panama, upon receipt of the funds, the note stated a decryption key would be sent.

Hacking did not originate with malicious hoody wearing criminals as popularised by media, but with people tinkering with technology out of curiosity and learning how to improve and exploit systems. This era was a time of tinkering with technology, seeing how it worked and what it could do, and although against the law, much of this hacking appears not to be malicious. This curiosity in technology and how it worked eventually lead them to committing cybercrime. Those involved in phone phreaking, as opposed to being mysterious criminal hackers, started out with an interest in how the phone systems worked and were fascinated with how the frequency and tonal changes could instruct the telephone network to place calls. Similarly, rather than being created by some ominous shadowy hacker of fiction, the Morris worm started with a university student allegedly wanting to measure the volume of the ARPANET. The first known instance of ransomware, which took advantage of the interest in AIDS research and was delivered on floppy disks via post, was a precursor to ransomware crime activities to follow. These crimes against or enabled by technology existed before the Internet as we know it today and impacted both telephone and computer systems. As the twentieth century progressed, hacking and technology compromises became less about curiosity and learning and more about having malicious intent.

## Key Takeaways

- The term hacking, when related to technology, is thought to have originated with model train enthusiasts at MIT in the 1950s.
- As technology developed in the twentieth century there was a cohort of curious people who hacked systems to see what they could do and how they could be exploited.
- A precursor to the Internet, ARPANET, was accessed by a variety of curious youths wanting to see how big it was or what was stored there.
- The first ransomware was sent via floppy disks in the post.

*Chapter Three*

# END OF THE 20TH CENTURY AND Y2K

'The Y2K Scare was a phenomenon at the turn of the 21st century where computer users and programmers feared that computers would stop working on December 31, 1999.'– Kirsty Best[1]

As the twentieth century was drawing to a close, concerns rose over the Y2K or Millennium bug. Technologists were concerned computers would stop working in the year 2000. Phone based crimes continued with a criminal group called the Phonemasters and, the social engineer, phone phreak and hacker, Kevin Mitnick was charged and imprisoned for various computer-based and wire fraud crimes. Also, at the end of the twentieth century, a group of Californian based teenagers took advantage of vulnerabilities in restricted US government networks. The late nineties also saw freeware publicly shared malware impact AOL, creating the first use of the term phishing which described the cybercrime campaign perpetrated against AOL users and, a new computer virus spread via email infect Microsoft Word documents.

Although not cybercrime, in the interests of providing a more enhanced picture of the world of computing in the nineties and to better understand the cybercrime landscape of the time, it helps to share an overview of the Y2K bug. As computers were evolving in the 1960s, data storage was extremely expensive, so to save storage space software was coded to show years with two digits. That meant, for example, that the year 1960 was saved as '60' and the year 1975 was stored as '75'. This caused concerns as the century was ending, as many agencies relying on computers or computerised technology, realised that the computer programmes would see the year stored as 'oo' as 1900 instead of 2000. It was widely believed that all computers would stop working or malfunction badly at this point. Fear spread about the Y2K bug implications which included worry that the bug would cause hospitals to lose the use of vital computerised equipment, planes to fall from the sky and power plants to shut down.[2] There was public speculation about the Y2K bug and organisations spent a large amount of time and money working out how to prevent the computers failing as the century ended[3].

During all the preparations for the Y2K bug, criminals continued to run cyber enabled scams and exploit computer networks while law enforcement continued to face the challenges these criminal activities posed. Between 1994 and 1995, for example, a criminal group that the USA Federal Bureau of Investigations (FBI) named the Phonemasters gained unauthorised access to several businesses including the telecommunications companies Sprint and AT&T as well as the credit reporting agency Equifax. The Phonemasters were responsible for downloading confidential information about the customers of the businesses they breached, creating their own telephone numbers and, stealing credit card details. The US Federal court authorised the FBI to use the apparently first ever official data tap to provide them with digital surveillance of the criminals' activities. This tap, a type of keylogger, gave the FBI access to the keystrokes of the Phonemasters. Using this data tap the FBI captured evidence of the criminal group exchanging stolen credit card credentials. In 1995, law enforcement finally caught up with former phone phreak turned social engineer, Kevin Mitnick, who was arrested and charged for his computer and wire fraud activities.[4] The main people behind the Phonemasters group were convicted of theft, possession of unauthorised devices and, unauthorised access of restricted systems, in 1999.

Hackers and social engineers like Kevin Mitnick used their own skill and abilities to commit crimes, however there were people who wanted to be hackers, who lacked these technical and social engineering abilities. In 1997 for example, freeware malware was released that allowed unskilled 'wannabe' hackers to target users of America Online (AOL). This freeware was called AOHell and it exploited vulnerabilities in the AOL platform[5] to create faked messages in chat forums disrupting the legitimate messages with spam, downloading files without paying, and scamming credit card and AOL credential details from AOL users. AOHell credential scams were the first to be known as phishing campaigns and the name originated with the crimes committed using this free malware. This is where the terms 'script kiddies' and 'phishing' enter the vocabulary, with people who uses the codes others write to commit their crimes against or enabled by technology as the former, and spam messages used to social engineer credentials from others, as the latter.

In 1998 criminals systematically exploited vulnerabilities in networks running the Sun Solaris operating system. These exploits gave them access to sensitive data in over five hundred restricted US Government and private computers. The crime campaign was referred to as Solar Sunrise in reference to the Sun Solaris systems it was exploiting and targeting. Due to the political environment of the time, the US Government originally attributed the attacks to Iraqi nationals, but later discovered the crimes were being committed by a group of Californian teenagers[6] led by Ehud Tenenbaum (otherwise known as 'The Analyzer'). They were discovered and identified after they sent the stolen data to themselves. The other two teenagers behind this were discovered and identified because they had sent the stolen information to their own accounts using their home computers.

The last year of the twentieth century introduced the Melissa virus to the computing world. Using a combination of social engineering and malware, the Melissa virus infected Microsoft Word documents and spread itself automatically by emailing out to the first fifty email addresses[7] in the compromised computer's Outlook contacts list. The email carrying the malware had the subject line that included the words 'important message' and the body of the message included the words 'here is that document you asked for'[8]. This social engineering technique enticed recipients to open the attachment, which resulted in the recipient's computer becoming infected. At this time, the Melissa virus was thought to be the first to be delivered via an emailed attachment. The Melissa virus was released by David L Smith and he was charged and sentenced for the disruption and expense his malware campaign caused.

Also in 1999, fifteen-year-old Jonathan James exploited a vulnerability in the restricted computer systems of the US Department of Defence and installed a backdoor into the network. A backdoor in terms of cybercrime is computer code that is placed or used by a criminal so they can gain unauthorised remote access to a network or a computer. James, whose hacker name was Comrade, intercepted confidential messages from a variety of US government agencies as well as employee log in credentials. With this information, the teenager was able to steal software allegedly worth 1.7 million USD from the National Aeronautics and Space Administration (NASA). Not only had the young hacker accessed NASA systems, but also those of the Marshall Flight Centre, the telecommunications company BellSouth, and the Miami-Dad school networks. James was caught and charged, however due to his youth only received a light sentence. Sadly, he committed suicide in 2008 after being accused of conspiring with criminals to steal credit card information, which in his suicide note he denied[9].

The last decade of the twentieth century saw one of the most famous social engineers and hackers Kevin Mitnick arrested and charged for his crimes and for the first time in recorded history the FBI was authorised to use data taps to gain evidence against a criminal group. The nineties also introduced script kiddies and the first use of the term phishing to the world of computing via AOHell. Vulnerabilities in networks were exploited with the Sun Solaris systems being compromised giving criminals access to US Government networks and a teenaged hacker who penetrated the US Department of Defence systems and stole software from NASA. Microsoft systems were also targeted, with malware including the Melissa virus that infected email recipients via attachments. As for the Y2K bug, the century ended and the new one begun, and the computers kept going!

## Key Takeaways

- The end of the twentieth century brought with it the Y2K bug scare where there was concern that all computer devices would stop functioning at the turn of the century.
- The FBI used what is thought to be the first ever official data tap to provide them with digital surveillance of the Phonemasters' criminal activity.
- AOHell, the freeware publicly provided

malware, introduced the world to script kiddies and phishing.
- The Melissa virus infected Microsoft Word and Outlook applications and was thought to be the first malware delivered by email.

## Chapter Four
# CYBERCRIME IN THE 21ST CENTURY

"We Are Anonymous, We Are Legion, We Do Not Forgive, We Do Not Forget" – Hacker group Anonymous[1]

The start of the twenty-first century saw the evolution of hacking, social engineering and other cyber enabled crimes. It also introduced and popularised distinctions between types of hackers. Hackers were labelled according to their intent and ethics as either white hat, grey hat or black hat hackers. White hat involves hacking where a person is hired to legitimately locate vulnerabilities in networks or applications. Grey hat is a benign type of hacking that while unauthorised is not intentionally malicious and, black hat hacking involves unauthorised compromises of restricted computer systems for the purpose of crime. Unlike when computing started to become more mainstream in the mid twentieth century, there is less of the experimenting, inventing and almost fun aspects of tinkering with technology and seeing what it can do and a move to more malicious computer compromises. The twenty-first century has more of the organised criminal groups and other malicious threat actors using technology to commit crimes. As technology and the interconnected world keep developing, so does the opportunity for cybercrime.

Cybercrime campaigns are maturing in the twenty-first century and may not always be perpetrated by the people who have created the malware or social engineering template. That is because the brains behind these exploits and scams may not commit the actual crimes themselves but instead sell their skills, software and services to others. New types of compromises, viruses and cybercrime campaigns such as technical (tech) support scams and business email compromise emails were introduced in the twenty-first century, and hacktivist groups and criminal hacker associations were formed. Hacking as a term also evolved from the connotation it had with the MIT Railroad Club, to more malicious activity, but not all hackers are criminals and not all cybercrime is committed by hackers.

The start of the new century saw the fast spreading malware, the ILOVEYOU worm, go from its originating country of the Philippines to all the way across the world in May 2000[2]. The malware was written in Visual Basic, a type of programming language created by Microsoft. Once the malware installed on a victim's computer, and was activated, it would search for files on the infected computer and replace them with copies of itself. It also automatically self-propagated by sending malware laden emails to every email address in the infected computer's contact list. The ILOVEYOU worm also self-propagated by sending itself via Internet Relay Chat (IRC). IRC is a type of real-time text-based messaging system that was developed in the late 1980s. Using a combination of social engineering to ensure the recipients open the email, and malware, the ILOVEYOU worm campaign has been estimated to have caused billions of dollars in damages to impacted public and private sector agencies across the world[3].

Another worm, first discovered in late 2008 and targeting Windows operating systems, was the Conficker worm. This malware, unlike the ILOVEYOU worm, did not use social engineering techniques in email to spread. One of the known vectors for distributing the Conficker worm is an infected Universal Serial Bus (USB) thumb drive or other file sharing networks or devices. This malware can spread laterally in computer networks if it has infected a computer where the user has administrator privileges. The malware may also attempt to brute force or guess passwords. Variants of Conficker have been known to block Windows updates and patches, prevent access to cybersecurity websites and also download other types of malware. The Conficker worm is thought to have infected at least eleven million computers, including those owned both by individuals and corporate organisations world-wide[4].

Another cybercrime campaign that impacted businesses at the start of the twenty-first century was DDoS. Several large corporations were hit by a DDoS attack in the year 2000 which was attributed to a criminal going by the name of MafiaBoy. The DDoS was launched against large companies including Yahoo, eBay, CNN, Dell and Amazon. The perpetrator was discovered after he was found boasting on Internet messaging forums about his hacking prowess. The criminal behind these attacks was not the stereotypical shadowy hacker, but instead a fifteen-year-old boy called Michael Calce. The teen later explained that he had taken control of some university networks and used these to DDoS the websites. Calce was charged with over fifty crimes and was sentenced to serve eight months in a youth group facility. These days Calce is a respected information security professional and white hat[5] hacker.

The start of the twenty-first century also saw both formalised groups and loosely based associations of criminal hackers start to emerge. An example of these entities is the de-centralised hacker activist (hacktivist) group, Anonymous, which originated in 2003, springing out of the 4chan online community[6]. The 4chan site is an online forum where users can post images and create discussions anonymously. The 4chan image board was originally created by the then fifteen-year-old Christopher Poole[7] in 2003, who used the name of moot. Although the 4chan board is also used for benign activities due to the anonymity it provides it is often used by individuals and groups for malicious activity. Anonymous, one of the most well-known hacktivist associations, is known for using the Guy Fawkes mask as well as the logo of a faceless man. People identifying as members of Anonymous, form part of a collaborative leaderless collective, who work together against agreed targets. Another hacker group, the short-lived LulzSec, enjoyed a spree of criminal activity in 2011 mainly aimed at government and news or media websites[8]. In June 2011, LulzSec publicly teamed up with Anonymous for a campaign named "Operation Anti-Security", where they encouraged hackers to access, steal and make public any restricted information they could obtain from government agencies. Another criminal association, called the Lazarus group, is thought to have formed in 2009 and due to the nature of the vast array of cybercrime activities they have performed they are considered an advance persistent threat.

With the mainstream adoption of websites by businesses, web defacements, a type of virtual graffiti where sites are compromised and pages are replaced by a hacker's messages, increased. Web defacements tend to occur on websites with poor security[9], as they are easier to compromise. Websites primarily targeted by hacktivists for defacement are usually those run by political, corporate or religious associations. A news outlet reported in August 2019, for example, that a hacktivist group defaced the official web site of the New Zealand Institute of Directors.[10] Replacing the landing page with an anti-government message complete with an image of a person in a Guy Fawkes mask, the twitter account Vanda the God claimed responsibility. Interestingly, groups or individuals defacing websites tend to leave their contact details, such as email addresses and social media pages, on the defacement rather than hiding who they are. What is believed to be one of the largest web defacement campaigns in the history of the world wide web occurred in 2006, when the Turkish criminal known by his hacker name iSKORPITX compromised over 21,549 websites[11] in one go. Web pages defaced by this criminal all featured Turkish popular music, an animated medieval knight and, expletive filled statements.

Just as AOHell was freely distributed to nontechnical hackers, known as script kiddies, criminals at the start of the twenty-first century started to see the value in writing malware and selling it on the Dark Web[12] for other criminals to use. As well as malware being sold, criminals also started to share bank and website account credentials they had stolen. In the vein of the shared AOHell, often compromised credentials are dumped on publicly available web sites for anyone to see and exploit. This means that many separate criminal groups could be using the same malware or phishing templates in their cybercrime campaigns as they have bought them from someone else, making attribution quite challenging!

As well as defacements, exploiting websites and infecting networks with malware, the twenty-first century introduced a wide range of cyber enabled scams. Similar to the social engineering techniques used by Kevin Mitnick, criminals are using emails, telephone calls, websites and text messages to trick their targets into handing over their log-in credentials, bank account details and money. Emails designed to spoof senior managers directing finance teams to pay fake invoices start being noticed in 2012 and the scams, known as business email compromises, are so successful they continue to this day. Romance scams where people fake relationships to defraud money from their victims and technical support scams where criminals pretend to be employees of large companies to gain access to their victims' computers and bank accounts are rife. Cybercrime in the twenty-first century seems less about hacking networks than it is about hacking people.

The start of the twenty-first century also popularised the concept of black hat, grey hat and white hat hackers[13]. This terminology is based on old Western movies with the stereotypical good character wearing the white hat and the criminal wearing a black hat. Individuals involved in ethical hacking, the white hat hackers, do so legally with appropriate ethical considerations as part of their jobs. White hat hackers may perform system vulnerability checks, penetration testing (pen testing), and assess what networks, people or policies in a business can be exploited. They do this to support improvements in the security of a company's network and with the permission of the business. Like white hat hackers, the grey hats actively search for vulnerabilities in websites, networks and applications, but the difference is that although without malicious intent, they are doing this without the authority of the system owners, making their activity technically illegal. The black hat hackers are the criminals who are popularised by the hoody wearing stereotype. This group exploit vulnerabilities in networks for their own personal gain or other malicious intent or sell their created malware for other criminals to use.

Cybercrime and the concepts of hacking evolved in the start of the twenty-first century from the almost mischievous experimenting with technology of the previous century to an increase of threat actors with malicious intent. As technology develops and the world becomes increasingly interconnected, the opportunity and means to commit crime against or enabled by technology have grown. The advent of the twenty-first century saw the rise of selling malware as a service, new viruses, spyware and new versions of cybercrime scam campaigns. Hacking as a term evolved into three main types, black, grey and white. In the twenty-first century not all hackers are criminals and not all cybercrime is committed by hackers.

##  Key takeaways

- The twenty-first Century saw hacking evolve into a variety of forms.
- Hacking groups emerge, such as Anonymous, with members committing cybercrime campaigns in the name of activism.
- Criminals started to sell malware as a service to others to use.
- Not all hackers are criminals, with white hat hackers who act with authority to locate vulnerabilities in business networks, and not all cybercrime is committed by hackers, as there is an increase in selling malware as a service to non-technical criminals.

## Part Two

# CYBERCRIME - SCAMS

To demystify cybercrime and cyber enabled scams, and to work out ways to be aware of and mitigate them, it helps to understand more about them. It is easier to mitigate against scams regardless of how they are delivered, if the basics of them are understood. This section takes a closer look at cyber enabled fraud such as phishing, business email compromise and other scams using technology and social engineering techniques. Cybercrime encompasses far more than hackers and malware, with technology also being used to defraud people of money or information or to steal their credentials.

Fraud whether committed in person or via technology in cyber space is still crime and anyone can fall victim to it. Cybercrime is big business, persistent and there is no solely technical solution to prevent it. Technology based scams such as phishing, business email compromise, advance fee scams, sextortion scams, and tech support scams have success, in part, because they rely on common human triggers. Demystifying cybercrime, by providing explanations of what it is and how it works, can help people to understand it and better protect themselves.

The following chapters cover phishing, an activity and term which dates back to 1996 with the AOHell malware, business email compromises including a public domain case study, tech support scams and, an overview of a variety of other technology enabled scams such as the 419 scam.

## Chapter Five
# PHISHING

"We won't sit idly by when a crime is committed in the real world. So why should we when it happens in cyber space?" – Max Baucus[1]

Criminals swindling people into providing money for goods they will never receive, or to gain information from them about bank accounts or other personal information, are not new. With the advent of computers, the Internet and emails however these frauds can reach a further victim base than they could historically. This chapter looks primarily at an email fraud called phishing, and briefly summarises similar scams that occur via smart phone, called smishing, and, a type that can occur via any type of phone, called vishing.

The term phishing originates in 1996 with the AOHell scammers and it is a type of technology-based fraud where emails are made to appear as being sent from legitimate companies or familiar people in order to trick the recipients. There is nothing mystical in why phishing is successful, and neither are the perpetrators of this type of cybercrime shadowy figures in hoodies. Phishing emails exploit human psychology, using social engineering techniques, to trick the recipient into providing their account credentials or paying spoofed invoices. Common syntax in phishing emails, for example, is designed to make the recipient act fast without thinking their actions through, with their call to immediate action, spoofed believable entities and appeal to people to do the right thing. Phishing emails, for example, often convey a sense of urgency[2] which encourages recipients to make panicked hurried decisions, where they do not take the time to think whether the message is legitimate.

Successful phishing emails rely on being believable, playing to emotions and the false sense of security of the recipient. These scam emails whether they are baiting for credentials, money or intellectual property, rely on being believable, they spoof trusted brands or people and relate to everyday topics such as invoices, correcting log in issues or post deliveries. Phishing emails play to emotions with subject lines designed to scare or promote a sense of urgency in the recipient, or by cajoling or encouraging the recipient to do the right thing and click the link to fix a payment for example. Phishing emails also have success as end users may have a false sense of security believing that spam filters will block all malicious emails, or maybe having an over confidence in their own abilities to spot scams. Criminals send, or use bots to send, bulk phishing emails that they know will have success somewhere as so many are sent.

An example of a phishing email is in the following image, with a not terribly believable or imaginatively named fake company, "Australian Packaging Pty Ltd" advising that an invoice is overdue. The email had an attachment that stated the person needed to log in to their Microsoft Office account to view it. This email scam is a phishing email to steal credentials for an individual's or business' Microsoft O365 credentials. Phishing emails like this can be successful due to the threat of bringing in a solicitor and because it states there is a large amount of money owing. The recipient of the email may open the attachment and log in to view it, because they are confused about the invoice, or because they are fearful that they do have this debt.

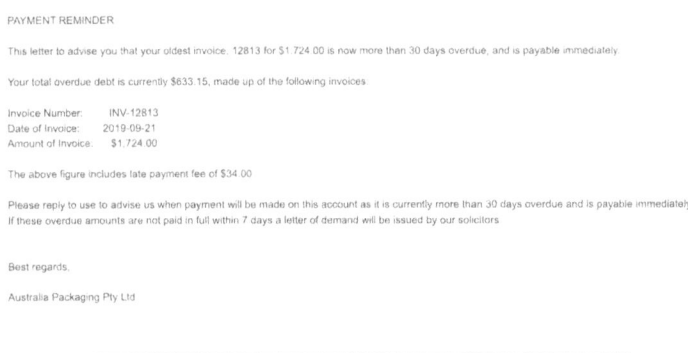

*Credential phishing email with a fake invoice*

A phishing email created to appear as if from the Australian Government's MyGov, however, is a lot more believable. The following image shows this phishing email that promises a tax return if the recipient verifies their identity from the provided link.

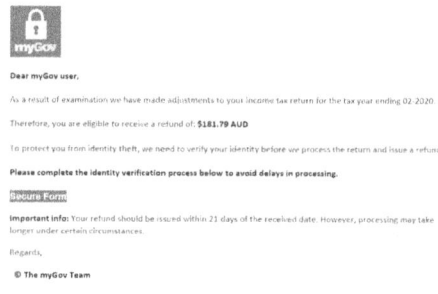

Credential phishing spoofing the Australian Government

Targeted scam emails however, known as spear phishing, are not bulk mail-outs to a mass of random email addresses but more specifically tailored personalised scam emails sent to specific recipients or businesses. Spear phishing uses information that criminals have often gleaned via open source intelligence (OSINT) such as scraping social media sites for email addresses and phone numbers and researching targeted individuals or organisations online. In this Internet age, there are people that share a lot about their lives online, there are data base breaches and often businesses in the need to promote their wares share a lot of information about themselves on their websites, all of this is a treasure trove for criminals.

While phishing is often thought of as an email-based scam, this crime is not just perpetrated via email. With the increased interconnectivity of the world, criminals can also approach their potential victims via social media in comments or direct messages, phone calls ('vishing' – voice phishing) as well as text messages ('smishing' – SMS phishing). Criminals will often use automated dialling and recorded responses for vishing, so that they can attempt to scam as many people as possible, just as in phishing emails. At times however, the criminals may make the calls themselves and spoof legitimate organisation, such as in tech support scams, to defraud the target of money or account credentials.

Smishing can easily catch people out, just as phishing does, as it uses the same psychological triggers such as playing to emotion, believability and a sense of urgency. Although people are becoming more aware of phishing they may not be as wary of similar tactics being used in phone text messages. Smishing text messages may contain links to malicious websites or encourage the user to download a specific app that masquerades as a genuine programme but is designed to steal personal information or record and send logs of calls and messages made on the device. Criminals may also use smishing to scam phone owners into providing their credit card details, passwords or bank account information, as they believe they are responding to a legitimate company such as an online retailer, telecommunications company or financial institution. Text messages used to lure potential victims may include topics such as bank accounts will be locked if the message recipient does not log in via the supplied link, or even congratulating them on winning a major lottery prize which they have to supply personal information and bank or credit card details in order to receive.

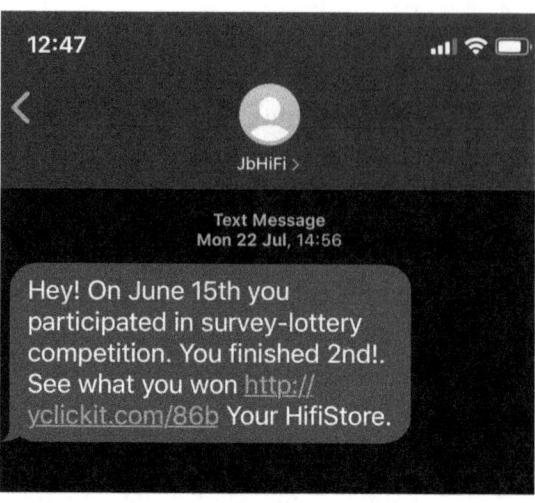

Example of SMS phishing [image credit Chris Macleod]

Voice phishing, or vishing, uses just the same strategies as both phishing and smishing, and exploits human psychology for success. As people become more aware of phishing and other email scams, criminal groups innovate to find new ways to defraud consumers and users of technology, and vishing is one of these. An example of vishing that has occurred in Australia is where the criminals pretend to represent the Australian Government's taxation office and inform the individual who answers the phone that they have a tax debt and must repay it or will be immediately arrested. Interestingly, the scammers ask for these debts or fines to be paid by gift cards, sadly people are still defrauded into thinking this is a genuine request for payment even though the genuine Government agency would not request a payment in gift cards.

Common phishing scams attempt to gain log-in

credentials of their potential victims or encourage files to be opened or sites visited that place malware on the recipient's computers. These compromised accounts are often mis-reported as hacked, but in reality, it is more trickery than hacking. Phishing scams may also be used to set up a bigger scam, once criminals gather intelligence from a scammed person, they can use these details to go for bigger scam attempts, such as business email compromise campaigns. With details derived from signature blocks, or from logging in as one of their credential compromised victims, criminals can send emails as the person whether spoofed or via the victim's compromised account to attempt to fool other employees of a business. Media may report on companies or individuals compromised by credential phishing as having been hacked, however it is not computer hacking if the victim has supplied or the details to the criminal themselves! Hacking relates to using code to exploit vulnerabilities in restricted networks to gain access, whereas phishing is a type of fraud that relies on criminals masquerading as a trusted entity or known individual to obtain credentials, data or money.

Phishing, smishing and vishing are all types of frauds that use technology to convince their targets to freely provide information about themselves, their bank accounts or their passwords. As individuals become more aware of email scams, criminals will continue to innovate to find new ways to scam people, such as smishing and vishing. It is important to note that attempting to defraud people by pretending to be a representative of a well-known company is not a new phenomenon even though in the modern world this type of fraud is usually perpetrated by use of technology. Successful phishing, smishing or vishing fraud rely on appearing believable from a such as from a well-known company, playing to emotions with sense of urgency or creating fear, as well as any false sense of security in the recipient whether they trust that technology will protect them from scams, or they believe they will never be scammed. Fraud is an ancient crime, but technology means the perpetrators do not have to be anywhere near their targets to achieve results.

## Key Takeaways

- The term phishing dates back to 1996 with the AOHell scammers and fraud is not a crime type that is reserved to technology,
- Successful phishing emails rely on being believable, playing to emotions and the false sense of security of the recipient.
- Phishing, vishing and smishing are all types of fraud that rely on criminals masquerading as a trusted entity or known individual to obtain credentials, data or money.

*Chapter Six*

# BUSINESS EMAIL COMPROMISE

"Business email compromise (BEC) is rapidly increasing, defrauding organisations out of millions of dollars' worth of funds every year and requiring little in the way of technical expertise" – Mansfield-Devine (ed)[1]

Business email compromise (BEC) is a type of email scam where, for example, a message is sent purporting to be from a high-level employee requesting that an invoice be paid urgently. In 2012, when this type of email-based crime first came to the attention of information security professionals, it was often referred to as wire transfer or CEO fraud, because of the type of payment the emails requested and the employee level spoofed. As the BEC scams continued over the years they have evolved to encompass not just attempting to defraud funds from companies but also to stealing intellectual property such as research data. BEC emails may be sent from compromised legitimate employee accounts or from spoofed accounts. Spoofed email accounts are designed to trick the recipient into believing the message is from a legitimate company or someone they know.

Spear phishing emails that aim to trick the recipients into providing their email log-in details are often a precursor to BEC scams. For example, once the criminals have the email account credentials of a company employee, they will use the account to send emails to others in the company or to a client of the company to request payment of an invoice. As the email is coming from a legitimate employee account, it bypasses normal phishing filters and adds credibility to the message. BEC campaigns are carefully planned and targeted with criminals doing intensive research on their intended victims.

Criminals who defraud people with BEC, are adept at open source intelligence (OSINT), scouring publicly available news, company information and social media sites to gain enough information to know who to target and what to say to be believable. The twenty-first century's phenomenon of over sharing on public social media sites and all the information displayed on company websites abut executive level employees, is a treasure trove for criminals. Armed with their well-researched information, the criminals will then target an individual from the researched business with a spear phishing email. This is done with the aim of tricking the target into handing over their email or corporate account credentials. If successful, the criminals will then add rules into the victim's email application to forward messages to themselves, and to delete any trace of the mail forwarding. Biding their time, the criminals will observe email interactions between employees and internal and external stakeholders as well as observe any invoices that go via the employee's email. The criminals will then carefully craft an email purportedly from a company CEO, either from the compromised account or from a spoofed account, to request payment of an urgent invoice. From their intelligence gathering they will know when the senior level employee is absent and will time these email requests for these times to add credibility to their messages and to make it harder for people to check with the CEO to see if the request is legitimate.

The CEO based BEC scams all have a similar template, with the email being brief, requesting urgent action to make a payment, stating that the sender is busy, away or in a meeting and cannot be contacted, and ends with sent from my iPhone. Another version of the CEO frauds is where the original email contact, instead of asking for a payment to be made, asks the email recipient if they are busy, or if they could urgently provide assistance. Once the email recipient replies, the criminals know their target has taken the bait, and then they request payment to be made, or even electronic gift cards to be bought for them. These CEO BEC scams always promote a sense of urgency to encourage the recipient to act fast which prevents them from stopping to think if the request is genuine or not.

An example of a CEO BEC is from 2018 when a

branch of the film company Pathé was reportedly defrauded of over 19 million euros. The BEC scam, that cost two people their jobs, and lost a large amount of money for the company, started with an email sent to the Pathé Netherland's CEO on 8 March 2018 spoofing the CEO of the parent company in France. The email message asked if they had been contacted by the consulting firm KPMG. The Pathé Netherlands' CEO forwarded the email to the Netherland branch's Chief Financial Officer (CFO). A second email arrived, again spoofing the parent company's CEO in France, stating that the company is working on a strictly confidential financial transaction with a business in Dubai. The message emphasised the need to keep the matter confidential and that all email replies should only be made to the French CEO's personal email address, which was the address the emails were being sent from. This was a very stealthy move on the part of the criminals, as it discouraged the CEO and CFO in the Netherlands from talking to anyone else in the company about it, and also meant that they were unlikely to email the real French CEO, as they were told to only email the personal address.

A third email soon arrived requesting € 826,521 to be paid, to whom the scammer said was an employee of KPMG Canada, for the beneficiary Towering Stars General Trading. The CEO in Netherlands emailed back to ask if this should be done with support from the company's supervisory board but was told by the scammer that it would be handled, and that they did not need to involve the board at that stage. The Dutch CEO apparently then emailed the CFO remarking the request was strange. The next day they received another email stating that the purchase in Dubai was going ahead and that a further 10% payment of the total cost had to be paid. The email had an attachment that contained names and signatures purportedly of the French CEO and other shareholders.

The second transaction was for €2,479,563 and when the Netherland's CEO asked the scammer if they could talk over the phone about the payments was told it was against KPMG policy to do that. The email chain was then forwarded by the Dutch CEO to the CFO who replied that the process is curious. Further payment requests were made and paid, and the emails contained assurances that the transaction was legitimate and that the funds would be paid back once the acquisition had been made, however at the final request, the Netherlands branch had to use money from the parent company to make the payment on 27 March, which was when the parent company started to ask questions. By the time the scam was discovered a total of €19,244,304 had been paid to the criminals.

This BEC scam stole a large sum of money from the company that was never recovered, and cost two senior executive employees their jobs. Sadly, although both the Dutch CEO and CFO appeared to be questioning the validity of the emails, processes and transactions, they continued to pay the requested amounts and interact with the scammer over email right up until the parent company started to ask questions about the payments.

Another type of BEC scam aims to steal intellectual property or information rather than money. These can occur after the criminal's compromise or spoof a senior level employee's email account and request sensitive information from the businesses' Human Resources, Research and Development, or Payroll teams. Inversely, there are also BEC scam campaigns, where the criminals provide information rather than request it. Payroll scams are an evolution of BEC emails where a compromised or spoofed employee account is used to contact the businesses' pay team to request changes to the bank account the employee's salary is paid to. If successful, the employee's pay would be transferred to the criminal's account rather than to the account held by the legitimate employee.

In this variant of a Business Email Compromise (BEC) scams, criminals email their target, usually someone from a HR or pay team, pretending to be an employee who requires help to change bank account details in the payroll system. The scammers will have already done their research in regards an employee to spoof, usually found on company websites or social media. Like other BEC campaigns these scam emails can bypass technical controls as they are either using a compromised account of the actual employee or have created an account on a free email service so the name and email address match. As this is a new variant of BEC, it also can bypass any warnings or training about BEC as the criminals are not asking for invoices to be paid or money transferred.

The payroll scam emails are usually brief, fairly polite and have a sense of urgency as they articulate the need to have their bank details changed before the next pay day. They are often initiated with a query about the process to change bank account details and confirming when the next scheduled pay would be. Once a target takes the bait and responds, the scammer will follow up stating they are unable to change the details themselves because they are away from a computer and ask the payroll team member to assist them. If a payroll scam is successful, the genuine employee's pay will end up going to an account controlled by the criminal.

BEC scams can take a variety of forms such as faking company invoices to request payment, faking a company's CEO email to request a supplier be paid and, faking a senior level employee asking for specific restricted business or research files be emailed to them. BEC scams are well researched, personalised and create a sense of urgency and secrecy. Criminals take care to make their initial email approaches for BEC believable, using the target's names and including a personalised greeting. As the emails rarely contain links or attachments, they can evade many technical solutions, making a solely technical mitigation impractical. The sense of urgency in the messages and the fact they appear to be from senior executive employees make them difficult for the recipients to ignore.

## Key Takeaways

- Business email compromise is a type of email scam where a message is sent purporting to be from a high-level employee requesting an action to be done urgently.
- BEC emails can bypass technical controls as they are either using a compromised account of the actual employee or have created an

account on a free email service so the name and email address match.
- The sense of urgency in the messages and the fact they appear to be from senior executive employees make them difficult for the recipients to ignore.

## Chapter Seven
# TECH SUPPORT SCAMS

> " It might seem obvious that computer scams play off the public's general lack of knowledge" - Tabron[1]

Technical (tech) support scams, also known as remote access scams, use social engineering techniques to trick people into believing they have malware on their computer. The criminals will then persuade their intended victim to install remote access software providing them with access to their target's computer. Once the scammer has access, they will open different files and parts of the operating system or system event logs to persuade the victim that their computer has a virus and needs to be fixed. The criminals will request payment to fix the computer, sometimes in credit card payments and at other times in purchased gift cards. They may also steal data such as passwords and banking credentials while they have access to the victim's computer. Tech support scams can be initiated a variety of ways including cold calls from fake tech support personnel pretending to be from well-known telecommunications or software companies, via adverts that appear high up in search engines after exploiting search engine optimisation (SEO) techniques, or in browser pop-ups in compromised web sites.

Tech support scammers are known to cold call people and state that they are calling from well-known software or telecommunication companies to tell the potential victim they are calling as they are aware that a virus has been located on their computer. Another way the tech support scammers find potential targets is by creating web popups or malvertising to state that the computer has viruses and suggests the person to contact a phone number or install software to fix the problem. If the scammer can convince their target that they are indeed technicians from a trusted company, they will then ask their intended victim to log into their computer and download a legitimate remote access application. The remote access software itself is not malware. The criminals will state that they need this to access the target's computer from their secure server to fix the computer for them. Once they have access, they will show the target some log files that are a normal part of the computer's operations and state that these are an example of the malware. The tech support scammer will then request payment to fix the computer or an ongoing subscription payment to protect the computer. If a potential victim becomes suspicious about the alleged computer fixes or questions the scammer, they may be met with abusive language, blackmail or threats.

Another version of this scam is where malicious advertisements known as malvertising, or pop ups appear on websites being visited. These popups use what may be termed scareware, that states that the computer being used has malware on it or suggests that the computer needs to be scanned for viruses and directs the person to call a number being displayed. A similar way that people are scammed by tech support frauds is where, exploiting search optimisation techniques, the advertisement on faked business websites of the scammers is displayed. These websites are using names very similar to the genuine businesses and take advantage of common typing errors made when typing the company names. Using search engine optimisation techniques, where websites are crafted with key words and other techniques to make them more noticeable by search engines, the scammers ensure their spoofed business websites appear prominently in website searches. People requiring help with their computer or software may be tricked into believing these sites are run by legitimate tech support companies.

*Tech support scam pop-up*

Once a user has been scammed, there may be a follow-up some time later where they are again contacted via phone, but this time the criminals state that the company is closing its business, so they wish to refund the victim. During the faked refund process the scammers then inform the victim that they accidentally refunded too much and then demand the victim immediately pay them back with gift cards. A variant on part two of this scam is where the scammers contact the victim to state they are investigators and they need help catching the criminals who scammed them in the first place and ask for money to help them do this.

## Key Takeaways

- Tech support scams use social engineering techniques to trick people.

- Tech support scammers are known to cold call people and state that they are calling from well-known software or telecommunication companies.
- Once a tech support scam has defrauded a target, there may be a follow-up some time later to the victim pretending to be law enforcement and asking for funds to help catch the perpetrators.

*Chapter Eight*

# OTHER CYBER ENABLED SCAMS

---

"The "Nigerian 419" scams are another example of how users are deceived into providing sensitive information with the hope of receiving a fortune later" – Almeshekah and Spafford[1]

---

Cybercrime is not just about hacking, malware and phishing; it also encompasses other types of criminal activity supported or enabled by technology. Just like any other crime type, anybody can fall victim to cyber enabled scams and there is no solely technical solution to prevent them. In this ever increasingly interconnected and computerised world It is important for everyone to be aware of, and protect themselves from, cyber enabled scams. When people become more aware of the types of fraud that can be enabled by communications technology, realise they are just another way to commit fraud and see there is no mystery to them, they may be more able to protect themselves from being swindled. This chapter provides a brief overview of a variety of different cybercrime such as the Nigerian prince scam, romance scams, sextortion scams and those that take advantage of taxation time or special holiday seasons. These are all types of fraud using technology as the medium to get to their potential victims.

The cyber enabled fraud campaigns known as the Nigerian prince, 419 or advance fee scams, take their name from an area that has had quite the reputation for scammers. These scams take their name from article 419 of the Nigerian Criminal Code that deals with fraud. This cyber enabled fraud has developed over the years however in its most basic form, the Nigerian prince or 419 scam email contained a badly spelled message, with poor English grammar, stating the sender was Nigerian royalty and needed assistance to get their money out of the country. The message would offer the target renumeration in return for sending the alleged Nigerian prince funds to help him transfer his money. This type of fraud is not new, and neither is it only perpetrated via emails or websites. Dating back hundreds of years, a fraud known as the Spanish Prisoner scam has so many similarities to the advance fee or 419 scams, it could even be seen as a precursor. In the sixteenth century, for example, letters were received by people in England from an alleged countryman who had been illegally detained by the

Spanish King[2], Phillip II. The scammer would explain that should the person pay the ransom to secure his release they would be rewarded financially many times over, and in some instances the letter promised the prisoner's daughter[3] in marriage! Other iterations of this scam involved the alleged prisoner needing money to be sent so they could bribe the guards to help them escape, and of course the money sent was never enough, and there was always a new story as to why more money was needed. These days, although the cyber enabled versions of these scams can come from any country and have different stories associated with the request, they still tend to be called Nigerian prince or 419 scams.

The following image shows an example of one of these 419 scam emails that was received in November 2019, showing that these scams are still going strong! In this example, the scammer first provides a fictitious account of their terminal ill-health, ensures the target sees they are trustworthy with their God-fearing nature, and explains that they want the recipient to help them by taking their substantial funds and using them to support their families, humanitarian work, or the 'poor children'. If the recipient takes the bait and responds to the scam email, they would then be provided further and possibly even more elaborate stories to keep them on the hook and to obtain their information, money or even bank account details. All for the purpose of allegedly helping the sender of the email dispose of their substantial treasure before they sadly die!

**Subject:** RE: I GIVE YOU MY 470.000€

Hello,
I don't think it's a coincidence that I contact. It is good that after several days of intense prayer that I do, this is how the Holy Spirit has guided me to you through Grace God. I give my possessions to an honest person and in the need. My name is Mrs. CSORDÁS JULIANNA of Hungarian origin and I have lived in CANADA for several years. I am suffering from a serious disease which is causing me certain death; it is the cancer of the throat which I have been trying to treat for many years, unfortunately despite the efforts of the doctors.
I have a sum of 470,000€ which I would like to make a donation to a trustworthy, honest person, a church or a humanitarian aid organisation, whether he makes good use of it to help his family or to start a new life and above all to help poor children. I'm giving away these funds for free to change your life. I donate this sum because the love of one's neighbor is the basis of all my Christian life. I would then like to know whether you are in favour of benefiting from this donation ?Once you get in touch with me by e-mail, I'll send you :
A certificate of authorization and declaration of property that will the subject of a registration in your name.
A Will which I have taken care to sign and which will be the subject of a registration in your name A deed of gift that I have taken care to sign and that will the object of a registration in your name The order of transfer of 470.000€ to your bank account A medical certificate proving my illness. Please contact me as soon as possible via my personal E-mail address if you agree to my offer to have the procedures for obtaining the € 470,000.
May God's peace and mercy be with you.
Widow Mrs. CSORDÁS JULIANNA.

---

*Example of 419 scam email – wealthy widow*

Another example of this type of scam is in the next image, where the email states it is from a Catholic priest, with a very large amount of money for a humble man of God, who is dying and wants to gift his substantial fortune to the lucky recipient of his email. The course of this scam would be, if the email recipient replied they would get a response from the pretend priest and there would be some toing and froing where the criminal gains rapport and the target's trust. Once trust has been gained, the criminal would then send another email stating he or she needs some money to help pay legal fees to have the money released. Of course, there is no fortune and a dying priest did not send the email, it is just another scam.

> Dear Beloved,
>
> I'm Reverend Father Gidoen Isaac, I was born in Brooklyn, NYC, 1945, I was ordained into the Catholic Priesthood.
>
> Please take your time to read this message, although we have never met before, this is no spam, It's a real message sent to you. I know also that you will be amazed at the level of trust that I am willing to place in a person that I have never seen nor spoken with.
>
> I have been a catholic priest for over 45 years. I had a heart surgery on the 20-06-2018 and the Doctors have just informed me that I cannot live longer; I had a serious bleeding after the operation. I have decided to will to you all the money which I deposited in my bank account the total sum of $5,970,000.00 (Five million Nine Hundred and seventy Thousand US DOLLARS).
>
> I want you to use this amount to make the world a better place for the poor and less privileged, help the needy and also help your family members. I took this decision because I was raised in an Orphanage so I don't have relatives and presently I'm hospitalized, where I am undergoing treatment. That's why I have decided to contact you so that you can
> make good use of the money which I will to you.
>
> Regards
> Reverend Father Gidoen Isaac.

*Example of 419 scam example – wealthy priest*

The criminals behind the advance fee or 419 scams may also use social media and dating websites to create connections with potential victims, and trick them out of their money, with stories of large amounts of inheritance funds being inaccessible due to being in war zones and requiring money to help them transfer the funds. This leads on to a brief overview of romance scams, which can start on dating or social media sites, and also contain imaginative stories of why funds are needed. This type of cyber enabled scam has the scammers create faked profiles on dating or social media sites where they lure people into believing they are genuinely interested in pursuing a relationship. The criminals put a lot of effort into grooming their targets to gain rapport and to get the intended victim to trust them. Once the target is well and truly hooked, the scammer will start asking for money. The requests may be for funds to buy plane tickets so they could meet up, or for an emergency that has befallen them or their family. The tragedy of these scams is that some of the victims refuse to believe they have been scammed and rationalise the situation, still providing money to the scammers in the hope that the relationship will become real.

Scams using phones to initiate contact with a target, including tech support scams as well as a type of phishing called vishing (from the words voice and phishing), are still types of cybercrime as they use technology to enable the fraud. There are also phone-based scams where the criminals state they are calling from a taxation department debt collection or investigation area and state that the target has a tax debt that must be satisfied otherwise the person will be arrested. The scammers request payment in gift cards or vouchers and tend to become abusive and aggressive if the intended target does not believe them.

Other scams, this time delivered by email, are called sextortion scams. These emails use social engineering techniques to trick the recipient into paying money to the scammers so that they won't release compromising videos of the target. Of course, no such videos exist, but the emails are well crafted and use credentials from previously breached passwords to prove legitimacy. The email states that the scammer has placed spyware on the victim's computer, captured them on camera watching pornographic material and will send the video to the target's friends, family and co-workers if money is not paid. Extortion emails in general terms are where a scammer threatens to release information of their target in compromising situations if payment is not received. The criminals use specific user information, such as passwords or mobile phone numbers, to add authenticity.

Although there are a variety of extortion email scams, the Sextortion emails are a specific type of extortion email where criminal actors are aiming to convince targets that they have intimate videos or images of them that they have 'hacked' from the target's computer, and subsequently demand payment to not release the images online or to the target's family, friends and work place. The emails often contain a password or other personal information belonging to the target to 'prove' veracity. The password or other personal information is usually gleaned from past data breaches. Personal information such as a user ID, password or phone number is noted in the e-mail to add a higher degree of both credibility and intimidation to the scam. The email accuses the target of visiting adult websites, stealing, cheating on a spouse, or being involved in other compromising situations. The e-mail threatens to send a video or other compromising information to family, friends and colleagues if the ransom is not paid.

dqwviviannetk@outlook.com to me

i am aware ▮▮▮▮▮▮ is your passphrases. Lets get right to the point. Nobody has compensated me to investigate you. You may not know me and you're probably thinking why you are getting this email?

i installed a software on the xxx video clips (porno) web site and you know what, you visited this web site to experience fun (you know what i mean). While you were viewing videos, your internet browser started working as a Remote control Desktop having a keylogger which provided me access to your display screen and web cam. Just after that, my software program collected your complete contacts from your Messenger, FB, as well as emailaccount. after that i created a video. First part shows the video you were viewing (you have a good taste omg), and second part displays the view of your web camera, & it is you

You get not one but two alternatives. We are going to understand these solutions in aspects

Very first option is to just ignore this message. Consequently, i will send your tape to every one of your contacts and then just consider concerning the shame you can get. Do not forget should you be in an important relationship, exactly how it would affect?

2nd solution is to pay me $1477. We will name it as a donation. in this instance, i will straight away remove your video footage. You could keep going on everyday life like this never took place and you never will hear back again from me.

You will make the payment via Bitcoin (if you don't know this, search 'how to buy bitcoin' in Google search engine).

BTC address to send to:

Scan the QR code with mobile to get the address

if you may be planning on going to the law enforcement officials, good, this email message cannot be traced back to me. i have covered my moves. i am just not trying to charge a fee so much, i want to be compensated. You now have 48 hours in order to pay. i have a special pixel in this message, and now i know that you have read this mail. If i do not receive the BitCoins, i will definitely send out your video to all of your contacts including members of your family, coworkers, and so on. Nonetheless, If i do get paid, i will destroy the video immediately. if you want to have evidence, reply Yeah! then i definitely will send your video recording to your 11 contacts. it is a non-negotiable offer therefore do not waste my time & yours by responding to this e mail.

---

*extortion scam email [Image credit Alex Kenley of Threat Vector Security]*

Some cyber enabled scams are seasonal, taking advantage of annual festivals such as Thanksgiving or Christmas, popular shopping days such as Cyber Monday or New Year sales and, tax return times to defraud people. Each major holiday season, for example, there tends to be a spike in cybercrime, particularly during large seasonal sales. The holiday seasons have an increase in gift giving, online purchases and deliveries. Which is all fodder for those perpetrating cybercrime. Scam emails or social media links offering too good to be true special offers for the season lure their victims to spoofed versions of well-known shopping websites which are designed to steal credit card and personal identity details. There is also an influx of spam emails and posts on social media offering the recipient faked lottery wins, gift card coupons and giveaways, for a small fee and some personal information!

Taxation time also gives criminals a basis to attempt to scam people, in this case by pretending to be tax agents chasing debts. One type of taxation scam is via telephone where scammers call and state that if a fine isn't paid the person will be arrested. The scammers then request for a credit card payment to be made, with the victim asked to provide credit card details, to avoid being arrested. Other tax scams involve spoofed tax government representatives or agent emails or text messages, these scams could be used for credential phishing, identity theft or to obtain financial details such as bank account numbers and log in credentials.

With the advent of Wi-Fi, and community groups, businesses and events providing free public Wi-Fi, there is an opportunity for criminals to exploit this service for their own gains. Be wary of free Wi-Fi, which are the publicly available hotspots that do not require any credentials to use, as they are as appreciated by criminals as they are by legitimate users. These public Wi-Fi networks can be used by criminals to send malware to anyone that connects to them. Additionally, if a criminal gets their device networked between the hotspot connection and the potential victim's device, they can intercept the transmission and relay it on after they have gained the information they want. This gives them access to bank account credentials, emails, messages and any account details that are being transmitted via the public Wi-Fi. This doesn't mean that public Wi-Fi cannot be used, just that it needs to be used with care and consideration to security.

Not all cybercrime is hacking and malware, as just as in phishing scams, many different types of fraud can be committed by means of technology. This chapter gave a summary of different scams delivered by email, phone and text message to get to their potential victims. With no solely technical solution, increasing awareness of different types of cyber enabled scams helps to increase mitigations to them.

## Key Takeaways

- Anyone can fall victim to cybercrime and there is no solely technical solution to prevent it, so a holistic approach needs to be taken to mitigate the risks of falling for cybercrime.
- Phishing emails rely on being believable, playing to emotions and the false sense of security of the recipient.
- Cyber enabled scams are not just delivered

via phishing emails, as criminals may use social media posts or messages, dating sites, phone calls or text messages to attempt to defraud their potential victims.

*Part Three*

# CYBERCRIME - MALWARE

Crime against or enabled by technology is less likely to be perpetrated by stereotypical hoody wearing hackers than it is by organised criminal associations, insider threats or Nation State actors. The days of curious students investigating and experimenting with new technology and hacking it to see how it works or to improve it have gone. These days, as fast as technology advances so do the crime campaigns and criminals that are exploiting it. As technology, interconnectivity and computing networks advance, criminals invent new ways to compromise them with malicious software (malware) that they have created themselves or bought from someone else.

Malware is an all-encompassing term for a wide variety of malicious code or exploits including adware, viruses, worms, trojans, rootkits, key loggers, ransomware and browser hijackers. Adware tends to be more annoying than dangerous, although it can slow computer processes and open browsers to other malware. Annoyingly, Adware can also create pop-up windows that do not close. Viruses are programmes that attach themselves to other applications and replicate when the applications run, similar to the way biological viruses work. Worms self-replicate and can destroy system and data files saved on a computer. Trojans are very dangerous types of malware that can steal banking and other account credentials, take system resources of a network, install other payloads and create a denial of service. A payload, in terms of cyber security, refers to malware that is sent to a computer or other smart Internet connected device, downloaded and installed without the user's knowledge.

Ransomware is a type of malware that infects computers, it can move laterally in connected systems, and encrypt files or lock users out of their computers, demanding payment of a ransom for the decryption of files or unlocking the computer. Browser hijackers redirect searches and send the user to the web sites the programme's creators want you to see, including phishing pages or those that infect computers via drive-by downloads. Both legitimate and spoofed company websites may deliver advertisements that contain malware, called malvertising, or downloading free applications may also install adware or spyware.

The following chapters will look at, and provide short explanations of, some malware types such as spyware and adware, trojans, key loggers, and ransomware. There is also a brief overview of denial of service attacks and botnets used to deliver denial of service attacks or malware. There is a large amount of ever evolving malware names, cybercrime campaigns and malware types used by criminals and the glossary at the back of this book provides more information on these.

## Chapter Nine
# DDOS AND BOTNETS

> "Distributed denial-of-service (DDoS) is a rapidly growing problem. The multitude and variety of both the attacks and the defense approaches is overwhelming" - Mirkovic and Reiher[1]

When criminals want to cause major disruption to businesses, without even being in the same country as their target, a Distributed Denial of Service (DDoS) attack is an obvious choice! DDoS is used for a variety of reasons, such as hacktivism or financial gain, and the people behind these attacks may not even have developed or delivered the malware themselves. Additionally as many computers are needed to create the network traffic to cause a DDoS, criminals infect the computers of multiple victims to act as their slaves known as bots. These infected computers, which collectively form a botnet, are not just used to deliver DDoS attacks but also may send other types of malware and malicious emails.

A DDoS , in basic terms, is a malicious disruption of a server or computer network caused by bombarding it with a massive amount of Internet traffic. This malicious network traffic either prevents legitimate traffic getting through or stops the servers responding to the legitimate traffic. In very simple terms denial of service attacks are like traffic jams for computers. The difference between a denial of service (DoS) attack and a distributed denial of service attack is that a DoS uses a single computer for the attack whereas a DDoS uses a large network of computers simultaneously bombarding a target business with network traffic. A DDoS attack relies on the combined communication power of many devices, so malware designed to infect, and control computers and other network connected devices is used to fuel the attack in a botnet. Criminals do not only use botnets to create their DDoS attacks, as they can also instruct infected devices to transmit malware via spam emails messages. The criminals behind DDoS attacks may not have created the malware but instead purchased it as a malware as a service (MaaS) and they also may buy a DDoS service from other criminals as a DDoS for hire. The outlay for a criminal to compromise and gain unauthorised control of multiple computers in a botnet to create a major DDoS or large malware campaign can be far less than the degree of disruption a DDoS or virus can create for a targeted business, making the use of botnets to create disruption a handy tool for criminals.

As a DDoS needs a massive amount of network traffic to be successful, the criminals behind this type of attack need to harness the power of a large network of online devices. Similar to how, in the year 2000, Michael Calce used the networks of various universities to launch a DDoS attack against the large corporations Yahoo, eBay, CNN, Dell and Amazon, perpetrators of DDoS infect computers and Internet of Things (IoT) devices to act as a hoard of traffic against the chosen target. Examples of IoT devices that may be used in homes are personal wearable fitness trackers and Internet connected televisions, while some commercial IoT include road traffic monitoring equipment, closed circuit television and security alarm systems. With IoT devices increasing and becoming more mainstream as technology evolves, criminals have a lot of IoT technology to choose from to infect and create their botnets! The infected devices, whether computers or other type of interconnected technology, are referred to as bots or zombies as they are controlled remotely by the criminal to send large amounts of traffic to the target via a swarm called a botnet, which is a contraction of the words robot and network.

Computers can become infected by botnet malware, via a trojan for example, when a user opens malicious attachments in spam emails, downloading non-legitimate software from non-official sources or by opening links in malicious popups or malvertising adverts on websites. While often the owners of the compromised devices remain unaware that they are aiding a malicious DDoS attack, their computers obey the commands the malware and criminals behind it have given them. A DDoS, because it is utilising an army of computers, also called botnets or zombies, that don't belong to the criminals, can be relatively inexpensive for the criminals but can cause major disruption to the targeted businesses.

There are two main ways that the criminals behind botnets control the infected devices, and give them instructions, either via what is called a command and control (C&C) server or with a peer to peer (P2P) network. The C&C server approach is the more traditional method where the server sends automated directions to the infected devices through some type of communications protocol. The malware that activated the bots remains dormant until a command is received from the C&C to commence activity. This method relies on a centralised control and is more vulnerable to being tracked by security researchers or law enforcement agencies. The peer to peer network technique is decentralised and relies on the bots sharing information with and updating each other rather than all bots taking commands from one location. This is becoming the more common approach with criminals using botnets, as it helps their activities to avoid detection.

When cyber security professionals talk about DDoS, they may talk about different ways criminals can perpetrate the denial of service. As an example, and without getting into too much technical jargon, some ways to cause a DDoS are User Datagram Protocol (UDP) flood, Internet Control Message Protocol (ICMP) flood and Synchronise (SYN) flood. In very basic terms, both UDP and ICMP floods refer to when a targeted server is sent an overload of UDP or ICMP packets making the server so overwhelmed by them that it is unable to respond. A SYN flood also target's a network so that the server is using all its resources in responding to the malicious traffic and is therefore unable to respond to any legitimate Internet traffic.

An example of a denial of service incident occurred in 2012, when DDoS attacks were launched against the websites of both the United Kingdom Home Office and politician Theresa May. These attacks prevented legitimate visitors to those websites and, the decentralised hacktivist group, Anonymous publicly declared it was in response to a proposed extradition of Wikileaks founder Julian Assange to Sweden[2]. In November 2012 a man was arrested in England due to his alleged association[3] with these cybercrime incidents. Another example of hacktivism, in this case allegedly to demonstrate that certain game console companies hadn't invested enough in cybers security, occurred towards the end of 2015. A hacker group calling themselves the Phantom Squad used the social media platform Twitter to share its alleged motivations to take down the gaming networks of two large companies, in a DDoS attack in a similar manner to another group, the Lizard squad[4] who had done this a year before.

Cybercrime campaigns using DDoS are not only used for hacktivism however, as they are also used by criminals to, threaten to or, hold systems at ransom until money is paid to them. For example, in 2017 a criminal group calling themselves the Phantom Squad[5], who may or may not have been the same Phantom Squad who were behind the campaigns against gaming systems in 2015, threatened businesses that they would launch DDoS attacks unless a ransom payment was received from the targeted companies by the due date.

Many large-scale DDoS attacks were reported in the latter months of 2016, with the botnet traffic being sent via a wide range of network connected devices and IoT, including computers, wireless routers and closed-circuit television (CCTV) cameras. Researchers investigating the DDoS attacks and associated botnets traced this activity to malware dubbed Mirai[6]. The Mirai malware was cleverly created as, although it was designed to scan the Internet for any vulnerable devices, it also avoided the IP addresses of major businesses and government agencies, thus helping it to stay undetected. When a vulnerable connected device was discovered, the Mirai malware would try to credential into it using a set of common administrator default passwords and brute force techniques. This is one of the reasons it is very important to change the default administrator credentials in wireless routers and any other technology that uses passwords. Once successfully compromised the device was then instructed by the malware to connect to the command and control server for instructions. The source code for the Mirai botnet malware was released to the public domain, allowing anyone with malicious intent to use it to create botnets from non secured or vulnerable IoT devices.

Botnets are not just used for DDoS attacks; criminals also may use them to send bulk malicious email campaigns, spread other malware such as trojans and, exploit advertisement monetisation. For example, the Zeus malware[7], also known as Zbot, was first discovered in 2007 and it initially was a banking trojan. Zeus was designed to collect bank account credentials from infected computers and then used the infected devices as a bot to send out malicious emails to further spread the Zeus trojan. Over the years the malware evolved to also infect compromised devices with other malware types such as the Cryptolocker ransomware.

An updated version of the Zeus malware was discovered by security researchers in 2011, and unlike its predecessor the new version, Gameover Zeus, used the decentralised P2P[8] approach rather than the C&C. The Gameover Zeus malware generated its own domain names to use as communication nodes for the bots. A basic explanation of a domain name is the unique name used to identify a website, such as demystifycyber.blogspot.com, which is the name used to identify the website that complements this book. The GameOver Zeus infected devices would keep searching randomly selected domains until they found ones that would issue them commands. An example of ransomware that was carried by the GameOver Zeus botnet, was the CryptoLocker ransomware from 2013. International law enforcement agencies collaborated in Operation Tovar and attempted to disrupt the GameOver Zeus botnet by identifying the domains being used by the criminals and redirecting the botnets to seek commands from servers controlled by a government entity.

Methbot was another botnet that was also not used for DDoS activities and it was first discovered in 2016. This botnet was different to most other types in that it did not use infected devices but ran on dedicated servers[9], called a Bot farm. It was an advertisement fraud botnet designed to create pseudo clicks and mouse movements as well as create fake social media accounts in order to take advantage of online advertising and video monetisation schemes. Another botnet malware, called Necurs[10], thought to be one of the largest globally, is known to distribute malware such as, the Locky ransomware, the Jaff ransomware and the banking trojan TrickBot to name a few.

DDoS campaigns use botnets to send huge amounts of traffic to the target systems. These attacks can be majorly disruptive to the targeted businesses but not create a huge outlay for criminals as they are using compromised computers of individuals or businesses or IoT devices to create the botnet traffic. Criminals behind DDoS incidents may not have created the malware for the botnets themselves as they may have bought it from someone else as a MaaS. Although DDoS attacks use botnets to create the traffic to overload the target servers, botnets are not just used to create DDoS attacks. Botnets are additionally used to automate sending spam or malicious emails and to deliver other malware payloads such as trojans and ransomware.

Key Takeaways

- DDoS attacks can cause major disruptions to businesses with minimal effort by criminals who are harnessing the transmission power of many compromised computers.
- DDoS campaigns may be used by hacktivists

to cause a disruption to targeted organisations, or by other criminals to demand a ransom in return for not attacking the networks.
- Three types of DDoS attacks are UDP, ICMP and SYN floods which all overload servers so that they are unable to respond to legitimate traffic.
- Botnets can be used to create DDoS attacks, but they can also be used by criminals to send spam emails or malware.

*Chapter Ten*

# SPYWARE, MALVERTISING AND LOGIC BOMBS

".. spyware ... disguised itself as legitimate Android applications to gather information from users" – Trend Micro[1]

This chapter covers three different types of unrelated malware versions and campaigns, known as spyware, malvertising and logic bombs. Spyware is an umbrella term for a variety of malware that, once installed on a computer or other smart device that connects to the Internet, stealthily collects personal information about the computer user. Spyware, such as adware, may collect information such as Internet browsing habits and other personal information about the computer and the user and forwards the data without the user's knowledge or permission to external recipients such as advertisers or data collection companies. Another type of spyware, called stealware, can redirect funds from affiliate links to the criminals behind the spyware. There are also types of spyware that can install other programmes without the computer user's knowledge and change the browser and security settings on devices. Spyware does not only infect computers as it can also infect smart phones. Malvertising, a contraction from the words malicious advertising, is sometimes confused with a spyware type, adware, but it is vastly different. While adware is installed on and impacts a victim's computer, malvertising has malicious code in legitimate advertisements, or in spoofed advertisements, on web sites and can impact any user that goes to that page and clicks the links. Then there are logic bombs, which are nothing to do with spyware or malicious code in advertisements. Logic bombs consist of maliciously inserted code in an application or database and are designed to execute a malicious event against the software, database or computer when certain conditions are met. All three of these malware types, spyware, malvertising and logic bombs can be used for malicious activity against computers and networks as well as the users of the technology.

Malicious spyware is created to hide on the device it infects, operate stealthily without making the user aware of its presence and, be difficult to detect. Spyware can infect a variety of operating systems and devices although Windows systems tend to be more easily infected. Computers can become infected by spyware from some types of freeware or pirated software, in malicious email attachments and, from accepting and clicking into malicious pop-up prompts that appear on websites. Computers are not the only technology that can be infected by spyware, as smart phones and tablet devices can also be infected by installing malicious applications that spoof legitimate ones. Different types of spyware can do far more than collect data on the websites a user visits, with some malicious spyware used to obtain more sensitive data such as email account credentials, financial account information and any files saved on the infected computer. Spyware operates without a user's consent or knowledge and the information collected could create both privacy and security concerns. Adware is an example of a type of spyware, and although not necessarily harmful in of itself it can make a computer more open to malware infection.

Adware is an application that is designed to push pop-up advertisements on to a computer screen usually via a web browser and it may not always be created with the intention of being malicious. Although not directly causing damage to the computer it infects, Adware, once downloaded, installs and spreads itself through the system, attaches itself to other applications and is inherently difficult to remove. The application, often a plugin or browser extension, may also redirect a person's web searches to malicious sites and create popup windows that can't be closed. A browser plugin is a type of computer application that works as an add on to give a browser additional functions, there are many legitimate types of browser plugins as well as the nefarious sort such as adware. Adware is often disguised as a legitimate application or it is designed to trick a person into installing it as a browser plugin along with seemingly legitimate free applications.

Different types of Adware may collect information about the websites a person visits, or it may alter the security and default settings of web browsers. Adware by virtue of how it operates, can slow the response rate of the infected computer and browsers. Because adware alters the security state of web browsers, the infected computer is more vulnerable to malware. Two examples of malicious adware are applications called adware.-CoolWebSearch[2] and Internet Optimizer. Both types of spyware are downloaded and installed on computers in a variety of ways such as when a person opens an adware infected email attachment, clicks on malicious spoofed sponsored links on compromised websites or downloads seemingly legitimate, but compromised, software. CoolWebSearch not only displays unwanted advertising pop ups on the infected computer, but also prompts the user to install fake application updates that may contain malware. Internet Optimizer, also known as DyFuCa interferes with the operation of Microsoft's Internet Explorer browser and redirects searches, broken links and incorrect web addresses to advertisement sites. The DyFuCa spyware also downloads other malware on to the infected computer.

Another type of spyware variant, dubbed stealware, is used to steal the payments from affiliate links. Affiliate links provide the identity of the person or website that has shared a business' advertisement and driven the traffic to that business website. Using legitimate affiliate links from genuine businesses can provide a passive income to the person or website signed up as an affiliate. Affiliate links provide income by rewarding the person or website for driving the customer traffic to their sites. Stealware[3] takes the payments that would normally have been paid to the affiliate and diverts them to the criminal who created the spyware.

Spyware does not just infect traditional computers as, with the increased use of smart phones and tablets for Internet connection and communications, criminals can see advantages in having their spying applications installed on smart phones as well. Smart phone applications (apps) that spoof legitimate software can trick users into installing them by being free and made to appear like well-known applications. For example, researchers from security firm Trend Micro reported in early 2019[4] on spyware, called MobSTSPY, in applications, that appeared to be legitimate, such as Flappy Birr Dog, FlashLight and Win7Launcher. The Trend Micro report also stated that the spyware MobSTSPY, can obtain a variety of personal information from the smart phone the malicious app is installed on. The spyware that infects smart phones can obtain the location of the phone, what is written in text messages and call logs. Smart phone spyware can also launch phishing campaigns by displaying spoofed social media pages designed to trick the user into providing their account credentials. This demonstrates that it is not just computers that can be infected and impacted by malware, as other smart devices are also at risk.

Just as adware can create advertising pop-ups that

direct users to malicious sites and downloads, malvertising also uses the concept of advertisements to deliver malware. Malvertising involves criminals installing their own malicious code into legitimate advertisements that are displayed on websites, or creating spoofed advertisements, that appear to be genuine, but lead to malware. This type of malicious code can infect computers when the advert is clicked on, in a drive-by-download, usually by exploiting security vulnerabilities in browsers. Malvertising may appear on non-compromised legitimate websites as it can be displayed via genuine advertising networks that cycle advertisements on websites. An example of a malvertising campaign is one called RoughTed[5]. First discovered in 2017, this malvertising campaign was coded to avoid ad blocking applications and evade many antivirus solutions while serving up malware to anyone who clicked on the advertisements. The RoughTed malware not only was able to avoid detection but also had the capability of push a variety of other malware to an infected computer, such as credential stealing applications, ransomware and adware.

A different type of malware, that does not infect computers from malvertising, adware or any other type of external malicious software, but instead is part of the original or updated code, is called a logic bomb. A logic bomb is a type of malicious code that is intentionally inserted into software being coded or administered by the person who embedded the code. Logic bombs are coded into legitimate software or databases without the knowledge of the other users or owners of the application or business. Logic bombs are designed to execute a specific function once certain conditions are reached. This type of malicious code does not self-replicate and tends to remain in the network in which it was created, which points to logic bombs usually being created by malicious insiders or disgruntled employees.

An example of a logic bomb incident was when a contractor at the Siemens Corporation, Mr. David Tinley, created an application for the company with a logic bomb inside[6]. The logic bomb was intended to make essential company spreadsheets to malfunction after a certain time. Tinley had allegedly created the logic bomb to ensure he would be rehired by the company to fix the repeatedly breaking spreadsheets! This worked for the first couple of years, with Tinley being called in to fix the spreadsheets every time they stopped working, so his logic bomb scheme went undiscovered for at least two years. The logic bomb was discovered after Tinley was away and provided the administrator credentials to other employees who discovered the embedded code. In July 2019, the then sixty-two-year-old, David Tinley pled guilty[7] to the subterfuge and faced a large fine, imprisonment or a combination of both.

These three types of malicious codes and campaigns, spyware malvertising and logic bombs show the diverse ways that malware can infect computers and networks, via piggy backed applications on freeware or pirated software, through malicious code on web advertisements, or coded into databases and applications by malicious insiders. Spyware applications are insidious, they collect and send information about the computer or other smart device and its user to unknown third parties. Spyware can be both a security and privacy threat and pave the way for other malicious applications or phishing. Spyware is hard to detect and may be ignored by anti-virus applications as they appear as if they are a normal part of the browser programming. Malvertising is malware delivered by malicious web advertisements and tends to exploit vulnerabilities in web browsers to install themselves and infect computers. Different to spyware and malvertising, logic bombs are malicious code usually created by a company insider and embedded into the code of databases and applications used by a business. Logic bombs act when certain conditions are met such as malfunction if an employee has been sacked. All of these are examples of cybercrime; however, they do not involve any mysterious masked hackers.

## Key Takeaways

- Spyware is a type malware that collects personal information about the computer user without their knowledge or permission and sends it to external recipients such as advertisers or data collection companies.
- Stealware, also a type of spyware, can steal the funds from affiliate links by diverting the payment to themselves.
- Malvertising involves inserting malicious code in legitimate advertisements, or serving up spoofed malware laden advertisements, on to websites as embedded advertisements

or popups, that can infect computers when the advert is clicked on.
- Logic bombs are types of code inserted into software and created to execute a specific function once certain conditions are reached, such as to cause a database to malfunction if an employee has been sacked.

*Chapter Eleven*

# TROJANS, KEY LOGGERS AND CRYPTOJACKING

"A cryptojacking site abuses the computing resources of its visitors to covertly mine for cryptocurrencies." – Musch, Wressnegger, Johns and Riek[1]

Anyone can fall victim to cybercrime and any computing device can be infected with malware. Nobody is immune to cybercrime, however the more we understand it, the more we are able to protect ourselves from it. The following is a brief overview of three different types of malware to demonstrate how diverse malicious software can be. This chapter looks at trojans, keyloggers and cryptojacking and provides some public domain examples of their use.

The trojan horse, more commonly called trojan, is

named after the ancient Greek story of the Trojan war and the fall of the city of Troy. Just as how the Trojan horse statue hid enemy soldiers, a computer trojan is software that appears to be a legitimate application or file that is actually hiding malware.Computer trojans are types of malware that may appear benign, even looking like and named similarly to legitimate applications, and are used by criminals to do a variety of malicious activities on the infected systems. Trojans are not the same as worms, as they cannot self-replicate, they instead rely on humans to interact with and distribute the malware by opening infected email attachments or downloading what appears to be legitimate software applications from the Internet but is actually malware.

There are many types of computer trojans, including those that are designed to gain remote access of the target's computer or network, steal banking credentials, send out emails with malicious links to spread the malware or, disable any anti-virus software on the victim's computer. The trojan malware may download from the spoofed sites of legitimate businesses, or on pages added to compromised websites, and installs itself on to the victim's computer. The trojan can search for specific information and credentials stored on the computer that relate to personal banking or other account credential information. Some trojans are created to redirect Internet traffic from legitimate banking websites to a spoofed version of the site that is operated by the criminals. There are also types of trojans that are used to spread a variety of other different types of malware to the infected devices. Some trojan types include backdoor, ones that create botnets to cause a DDoS incident, exploit, and banking trojans.

Backdoor trojans are designed to provide criminals with remote access of the compromised computer. Once a backdoor trojan has been installed criminals are able to send as the system owner, delete files, add other malware, and even use the computer to control and communicate with botnets. This neatly introduces the concept of DDoS trojans, that once installed on an infected computer or network, can be used to make the device part of a botnet to send massive amounts of Internet traffic to cause a denial of service. Trojans designed to exploit systems, target vulnerabilities in applications running on the infected computers and, banking trojans are created to access information stored on a computer or network to steal bank account information, credit card details, and the relevant account credentials.

A trojan from 2006, dubbed Storm Worm[2], infected computers via emails and had the intriguing subject line of "230 dead as storm batters Europe". This enticed recipients to open the email and click the link to view what they believed was the online news article. This trojan turned computers into bots that were instructed to keep spreading the malware via spam emails. Showing that criminals evolve their tactics to stay current, just prior to the 2008 Beijing Olympics a new version of the malware was sent with topical subject lines about major catastrophes in China.

A famous banking Trojan, Emotet, has been around since 2014 where it was first discovered targeting German banks[3]. The malware is primarily spread via spoofed emails, designed to appear as if from well-known known businesses. Using social engineering techniques, these emails express a sense of urgency to encourage the intended victim to open an attachment, view an invoice or validate a postal delivery. The Emotet malware can spread easily by accessing the recipient's saved email contact list and sending malicious emails to those addresses, it also can travel via a connected network of computers. An Emotet campaign that began in September 2019, for example, was spread via emails with subject lines such as "Payment Remittance Advice" or "Overdue invoice." Opening the attachments in the email started a small programme, called a macro, which downloaded the malware from a compromised site. Emotet is a modular trojan, in that while stealing banking credentials of a victim, it also delivers other types of malware to the infected computer such as ransomware or remote access Trojans.

Key loggers, either in the form of malware or a hardware device, allow criminals to spy on everything typed by capturing the keystrokes of the computer user. Key logging software may be spread via email, where recipients of messages may be tricked into clicking embedded links and installing the malware, and they may be downloaded as part of other types of malware. A banking trojan called, SpyEye, for example, contains keylogger software which criminals use to obtain log in credentials for financial institutions. Key loggers are insidious pieces of malware, that are not noticeable, can capture passwords and banking credentials as well as intellectual property, and they record everything typed on an infected computer.

Cryptojacking is another malicious activity, where

malware on a computer or on a compromised browser, uses the victim's computer to mine cryptocurrency. Virtual currency, also called crypto or digital currency, is a type of money that is not issued by a central or government authority. BitCoin is the most well-known and probably first cryptocurrency, however there are many versions of virtual currency such as Monero, Litecoin and Ethereum.

These three different types of malware or malware campaigns, trojans, keylogger and cryptojacking can all impact individuals, businesses and computing networks. A computer trojan masquerades as a legitimate application ,but, is malicious. Key loggers, that may be either a type of malware or hardware can capture every keystroke made on the target computer including passwords, bank account details and credit card numbers. Cryptojacking, using a device's computing power to mine crypto currency without the user's knowledge or authorisation can slow down the impacted devices. These examples, although different, are all types of cybercrime.

## Key Takeaways

- Computer trojans are malicious software that appear to be benign and once installed can steal banking credentials, download and install other types of malware and send themselves on via spam email.
- The Emotet Trojan targets anyone, whether individuals, businesses or government, and

the criminals behind the campaigns use social engineering techniques in emails to entice the recipient to open the malicious attachments.
- Keyloggers can be either software or hardware and are designed to spy on and capture every keystroke made on the target computer.
- Cryptojacking is when malware on a computer or on a browser is used to make the computer mine crypto currency without the user's knowledge.

## Chapter Twelve
# RANSOMWARE

"ransomware has become one of the biggest cyber scams to hit businesses" - Brewer[1]

Holding something or someone for ransom is not a modern crime, and ransomware is not a modern cybercrime. The concept of locking down a computer or files for the purposes of demanding a ransom payment from the victim first occurred with the AIDS Ransomware campaign of 1989. However, the 1989 campaign, spread by infected floppy disks sent via a physical postal service, was a very basic form of what this malware, and accompanying cybercrime campaigns, have become. In the twenty-first century there are two main types of ransomware malware, ones that lock down access to a computer or phone and ones that encrypt files. Locker ransomware, which tends to be most often used against Android devices, locks users out of their phones, tablets or computers, whereas the Crypto version encrypts all the drives, folders and files on the infected device. Ransomware can have a huge negative impact on businesses and cost corporations a large amount in time and money to recover their compromised systems.

Ransomware in the twenty-first century, unlike the 1989 AIDS virus themed version that was spread by floppy disks sent in the mail, is often spread via social engineering in phishing emails that encourage a recipient to open attachments or visit websites that infect the target's computer. Another way ransomware is spread is via compromised websites that infect computers when a user visits the site, in what is called drive-by downloading, or via social media messaging. In very simple terms, ransomware either locks down the victim's computer or locks down and/or encrypts the files of the infected computer, the malware usually displays a pop-up window explaining that the system has been locked and provides instructions on how to pay to regain control of the files. As both businesses and individuals rely increasingly on computers or smart devices, to store important information, the impact of ransomware to them whether they have up to date offline backups of data can be very high.

A ransomware campaign that may be the first to use RSA encryption to lock down the files of compromised computers occurred in 2006. An RSA key, named for its creators Ron Rivest, Adi Smanir and Leonard Adleman, is a type of cryptosystem used to encrypt and transmit data more securely. The Archiveus Trojan infected Windows based computers and encrypted all files saved in the My Documents folder. The victims of this ransomware were informed that if they made purchases from a specific online chemist, they would be provided a thirty-digit password to decrypt their files. Another ransomware campaign from 2006, used the GPCode trojan to encrypt files. The criminals behind this ransomware infected computers with a fake job application email. A twist on the ransomware theme arrived in 2007 with WinLock which did not encrypt computer files, but instead locked the desktop with a screen of pornographic images. The criminals demanded payment via premium SMS (short message service/text message) to unlock the infected computer.

A ransomware campaign, that locked down the infected computer and displayed a fake police notice, was known as Reveton or the Police Trojan. The Reveton malware was first noticed in 2012 infecting computers in Europe. The pop-up message was always personalised for the country the trojan was in. For example, in the United Kingdom (UK) the malware used a faked Metropolitan Police pop-up to inform the victim that they would need to pay a fine to have their computer unlocked and in the United States the message was a faked Federal Bureau of Investigations warning. The payments were requested in anonymised prepaid cash services like GreenDot money vouchers. The ransomware trojan infected computers from malicious codes that were inserted into advertisements which directed the victim to sites where the malware downloaded and installed on their computer. A person allegedly involved in distributing this malware, Zain Qaiser, was apprehended and, in April 2019 was found guilty and sentenced in a London (UK) court to six years in prison for his part in this ransomware campaign.

The Reveton malware locked computers rather than encrypted the files, however in 2013 an encryption ransomware appeared. The ransomware was called CryptoLocker and was carried by a Botnet named Gameover ZeuS. The CryptoLocker malware encrypted the files and any connected storage medium of an infected computer with a 2048-bit RSA key pair which was uploaded to the C&C server. The ransomware provided information to the victim that if a payment in Bitcoin or prepaid cash vouchers was not made within the provided due date, instructions would be sent to the C&C server to destroy the private key making decrypting the files extremely difficult if not impossible.

A new ransomware campaign in 2014, also sometimes called CryptoLocker but not the same campaign or malware as the one previously described, was discovered infecting computers in Australia. This trojan, also known as CryptoWall, used phishing emails pretending to be from the postal company, Australia Post, to trick the recipients into clicking a link to a page that downloaded the malware. As the malware was not carried in the email itself and the messages appeared innocuous, the emails were not being stopped by gateway filtering software.

First discovered in 2016, the malware named Petya, unlike other types of ransomware before it, was not a trojan and it encrypted the master boot record to stop the computer from booting. In very simple terms the computer's master boot record provides information to the system on where the operating system is so it can be loaded or booted up. The ransomware Petya self-propagated making it a worm, and it used the modified master boot record to show a spoofed check disk page and the ransom note, while it encrypted the disk.

A famous, and more recent, ransomware campaign from 2017, WannaCry, was thought to have infected over 200,000 computers in one hundred and fifty countries. WannaCry[2] included code that automatically scanned for vulnerabilities it could exploit and then install copies of itself. Ransomware causes major disruptions to businesses, with potentially irretrievable data, loss of time and money and, business downtime while recovering systems. Another ransomware campaign from 2017 that infected devices all over the world, was NotPetya. This infected computers mainly via malicious attachments in phishing emails and then moved laterally through the network exploiting the same vulnerability that WannaCry did.

In early 2018 a ransomware campaign called Gand-Crab was targeting Windows users and encrypting their files. This ransomware had an interesting idiosyncrasy in that it only infected computers that were not in Russia or the former Soviet Union. Researchers believe that this is an indicator of where the malware authors are based. This ransomware is also interesting in that it used an affiliate marketing model, also known as Ransomware as a service (RaaS). The RaaS model for GandCrab meant that the authors of the malware provided it to other criminals who, if successful, split the ransom paid with the GandCrab authors. Once a computer is infected by this ransomware the compromised machine displays a screen provides the victim information on where they need to go to have their files decrypted. One site allegedly displayed the following, polite message albeit with atrocious grammar: """WELCOME! WE ARE REGRET, BUT ALL YOUR FILES WAS INFECTED!".[3]

Ransomware, whether it locks devices or encrypts files, can have a large negative impact to businesses and cripple major services. Early in 2018, a hospital located in Indiana USA informed the public that their computer systems had been infected by ransomware, which was later discovered to be the SamSam malware. In this case the hospital paid the ransom, which was four BitCoins[4]. This ransomware is an encryption type and is known to rename all the files it encrypts to "I'm sorry". Unlike some other types of ransomware this malware does not spread via spam emails with malicious attachments, but it instead uses servers with open remote desktop connections. Another example of the SamSam ransomware also from 2018 was in Atlanta Georgia, when the malware crippled a variety of essential city services such as car parking and the court system[5]. The city did not pay the ransom, which demanded $51 000 (USD) worth of BitCoin[6], and struggled to recover lost official documents and services.

To avoid antivirus protection and discover new ways to trick people into installing the malware, ransomware campaigns, and the malware behind them, are ever changing. More recently for example, in May 2019, ransomware called RobinHood or RobbinHood crippled the government systems in Baltimore USA. Unlike other ransomware campaigns, Robinhood is not spread by spam emails but rather by compromised remote desktop services or dropped by trojans. This ransomware has what is thought to be a unique feature in that if the victim has not paid the ransom by the fourth day of the files being encrypted a further, 'penalty' amount[7] is added to the ransom.

In November 2019 another interesting ransomware campaign was discovered where the malware, which was coded in Pure Basic, went after servers. Researchers analysing the malware behind this campaign realised that it had remained undetected by mainstream antivirus scans for over three weeks since it first became evident, which is a rare instance in terms of antivirus applications and malware signatures. Once the malicious files have successfully installed and encrypted files on the infected device a ransom note is left on the computer desktop called 'YOUR_-FILES.txt'. Another interesting feature of this ransomware campaign is that the ransom note does not provide the payment details, instead providing details of how the victim may make contact to an email address to arrange payment and decryption. The victim is warned they have a certain time to pay, and if payment is not received on time the decryption key will be deleted. The email address uses the Proton Mail service which has a free option, is anonymous and encrypted. Due to the programming language used, the ransomware was dubbed PureLocker[8] by analysts at IBM X-Force and Intezer.

Ransomware impacts more than a business' data and computers, as the owners, employees and customers may also be hurt by the fall out. If a company cannot recover quickly from ransomware, it may lose both income and customers, resulting in business closures and job losses. Such a case sadly happened, in October 2019, to an Arkansas telemarketing company. The business suffered a ransomware attack and efforts to recover from it were unsuccessful. According to news reports[9] this caused substantial financial loss for the company and led to over three hundred employees losing their jobs.

As businesses become further reliant on technology to store, transmit and use information, the impact on them from ransomware increases. The twenty-first century ransomware has two main types, one that locks people out of their devices and another that encrypts the files or databases stored on the networks or computers. Ransomware can infect traditional computers and networks as well as smart phones and tablets. Ransomware can be hugely disruptive even when a business has offline up to date backups of their data. The time and resources lost for a business in fixing the infected networks and reinstalling systems and files can mean downtime in normal operations and a loss of income during that time.

## Key Takeaways

- The first recorded ransomware campaign was in 1989, with the malware in floppy disks delivered by post, rather than by email.
- Ransomware aims to either encrypt files of a victim's computer or lock them out of it and the criminals state they will decrypt the files or unlock the computer if a ransom is paid.

- Ransomware campaigns and the malware behind them are ever evolving to attempt to avoid antivirus scanners and find new ways to trick people or systems into installing the malware.
- Ransomware impacts both businesses and individuals and can result in job loss and company closures.

*Part Four*

# CYBERCRIME - THE PHYSICAL WORLD

Cyberspace is a jurisdictionally and geographically diverse extension of the physical world. Advances in technology and the Internet have benefited humanity in one sense but disadvantaged it in another. The ability to be able to communicate with someone who is in another country in real time from anywhere as long as there is a device connected to the internet means people can communicate with people across the country and virtually meet people from all over the world. It also means that people with malicious intent have the ability to do the same.

This part of the book discusses the leech over between the physical and cyber worlds, including a brief look at cyber bullying, cyber enabled child exploitation, data breaches and privacy issues in the digital age. The section concludes with a brief overview of some of the challenges law enforcement agencies may face when investigating cybercrime.

*Chapter Thirteen*

# CYBERCRIME - BULLYING AND EXPLOITATION

"Although technology provides numerous benefits to young people, it also has a 'dark side', as it can be used for harm" - Campbell[1]

While cybercrime often refers to malware, exploits or scams, there are other types of crime that can be enabled by technology. With the ever-interconnected world, the ability to hide online and the speed of electronic communications, crime that was originally only able to be committed in person is now also in cyberspace. Theft, for example, may be committed online instead of needing to be physically near the items to be stolen. Bank robberies also can be enacted in cyberspace instead of physically at the bank counter. Cybercrime however can do even more harm than negatively impacting the finances of a company or individual. There is another cross over between the physical and online worlds where stalking, bullying and child exploitation have all become a cybercrime issue.

With the anonymity the Internet can provide, people may be followed and messaged online by someone with malicious intent in what is termed cyber stalking. This type of harassment can begin with physical world stalking and then move to or include Internet stalking. This may include the victim receiving threatening emails from a person who hides their identity, harassing or intimidating forum or social media messages and sometimes phone calls. Because the Internet is accessible to many and has no geographical boundaries, there is no escape for the victim of online stalking or bullying[2]. This behaviour can become escalated and lead to actual physical violence when the cyber stalking activity escalates into the physical world.

Similar to cyber stalking, cyber or online bullying is malicious activity that can carry over from the physical world to cyber space. Examples of online bullying include where a person publicly posts online insulting, or hateful comments about a person, their behaviour, looks or personality. Just like bullying in the physical world, this activity can be hurtful, cause mental health decline and, sadly, has been known to be a contributing factor in victims committing suicide. Cyberbullying is not rare, in fact a survey, facilitated by United Nations International Children's Emergency Fund (UNICEF), found that in the thirty countries represented in their poll, one in three[3] young respondents reported having been a victim of cyber bullying.

Other heinous crimes enabled by technology

include child exploitation. Child exploitation, in this sense, refers to the sexual abuse, or sharing of images for illicit reasons, of people under the age of eighteen. The exponential development of interconnectivity and technology, such as the Dark web, peer to peer networks and live streaming has enabled criminals to easily share child abuse material whether for sale or for free distribution.

Technology such as smart phones, tablets and computers and communication forums such as social media sites being used by children have also increased the risk of children being groomed by criminals, encouraged to share inappropriate images or to even believe the criminal is a child, like themselves, and tricked into meeting them and then being abused or worse. With the availability and anonymity of the Internet criminals involved in child exploitation can remain hidden. This anonymity is a challenge for law enforcement, and the exponential growth of interconnectivity and technology will only increase the difficulty to locate, investigate and bring perpetrators to justice.

The online world has removed the tyranny of distance for everyone including criminals. Crimes, such as bullying, that traditionally were perpetrated in person have leeched into cyberspace. Targets of bullies are unable to find sanctuary from their tormentors as they can be surrounded by them in both the physical and online worlds. Child exploitation and grooming of underage people is enabled by technology and the anonymous nature of the internet, making these crimes extremely challenging for law enforcement to investigate.

## Key Takeaways

- Cyber stalking and cyber bullying are terms that have entered the twenty-first century vocabulary as the Internet and smart communication devices become part of normal life.
- Because the Internet is accessible to many and has no geographical boundaries, there is no escape for a victim of online bullying or stalking. Cyber bullying may lead to severe physical and mental illness and to the target fatally harming themselves.
- Intimidation using technology can become escalated and lead to actual physical violence when the cyber stalking activity escalates into the physical world.
- Child exploitation and grooming of underage victims is a risk with enhanced interconnectivity and advances in technology.

*Chapter Fourteen*

# DATA BREACHES AND PRIVACY

"Many companies face the risk of a data breach exposing stored personal information of customers and employees" – Gatzlaff and McCullough[1]

As the world moves increasingly to online transactions, cloud based databases and interconnectivity of smart cities and devices with the Internet of things (IoT), the risk of data being exposed increases. Recognising the seriousness of data loss many countries around the world are updating or have updated the privacy laws to consider how businesses are required to handle data breaches. With the evolution of technology created to increase physical safety, such as CCTV, facial recognition and traffic cameras, the concerns over privacy of individuals increases. This creates a huge responsibility to businesses and administrators of smart cities to ensure that the personally identifiable information (PII) of individuals is used and stored appropriately disposed of securely. It is also important to remember that data breaches are not just caused by cyber enabled activity but also by lost or stolen paperwork or storage drives. This chapter looks at some publicly reported data breaches and provides commentary on these from a cybercrime and security perspective.

A data breach not caused by criminals hacking into exploitable systems or using phishing to steal credentials to access databases, but rather directly through being lost while transported, occurred in 2005 and impacted customers of Citigroup. According to news reports at the time a box of back up tapes, from the computer databases, that contained customer PII such as names, addresses, account numbers, payment history and loan details of approximately 3.9 million people was lost while being transported[2] by a postal service. Also in 2005, sensitive data belonging to Time Warner employees was lost[3] while the backup tapes were being sent to a storage facility. Although these data losses were not due to criminal behaviour, it is useful to understand that data breaches are not just related to hacking or other computer compromises.

Data breaches that occur due to malicious intent to steal personal identifiable information, banking information, passwords, and other data can occur in many ways, however the main ways are via phished compromised credentials, exploited network vulnerabilities and malware such as keylogger. Personally identifiable information (PII) compromised by data breaches can impact the people whose information has been stolen, and also the businesses that have had their databases and files breached.

People whose information has been breached could become victim to identity theft, or have their information used in other cyber enabled scams such as phishing. Businesses that have suffered from a data breach can suffer from damaged reputations, loss of customers and income, subsequent cyber enabled criminal activity and, if they have insurance, increased premium costs.

The risk of data breaches will increase as the amount of data being collected and stored online increases. This is why it is important for businesses to only collect and store the minimum of information needed and to be vigilant about how data is collected, stored and later destroyed. Given it is not just cyber intrusions that can cause data breaches, it is also necessary for anyone transmitting information whether electronically or in hard copy take appropriate precautions against loss or theft.

## Key Takeaways

- As the world moves increasingly to online transactions, databases and interconnectivity of smart cities and devices with the Internet of things (IoT), the risk of data being exposed increases.
- It is important to remember that data

breaches are not just caused by cyber enabled activity but also by lost paperwork.
- Data breaches negatively impact both individuals whose information is compromised and the businesses that have been breached.

## Chapter Fifteen
# CYBERCRIME - THE PERPETRATORS

> " The easiness of communication, anonymity, and the accessibility of tools for illegal operations have transformed cybercrime into a global, fast-expanding and profit-driven industry with organised criminal groups ..."- Tatiana Tropina[1]

If the perpetrators of cybercrime are not hoody wearing hackers, who are they? To help unmask the hacker and demystify cybercrime this chapter takes a brief look at the various criminal types behind cybercrime campaigns. Perpetrators of cybercrime are a diverse cohort ranging from large organised criminal groups and those who develop and sell malware as a service, through to script kiddies, nation state actors, and hacktivists.

Cybercrime is big business and those involved may be part of large organised criminal groups.[2] These criminal organisations may be involved in diverse activities[3] and use cybercrime as a low risk way to generate funds for their enterprises. Just like any other business these criminal groups have a variety of employees with different skills to help them in their work. For example criminal organisations behind cybercrime may have a manager, an accountant, a coder, a promoter, a psychologist to help write social engineering scripts and a network administrator. These organised criminal associations may even have employees expert at intelligence gathering and data mining to help them find targets and make their approach seem legitimate. To help them find exploitable vulnerabilities in target networks they may even have their own version of pen testers. Using hidden forums and market places on the dark net[4], criminals may collaborate on projects and share information as well as sell their malware, expertise and services. Lacking their own expertise to develop software other criminal organisations, or even script kiddies, may purchase malware from these businesses. Script kiddies are unskilled in coding and carry out cybercrime using malware or malicious tools they have obtained or are employed to use.

These criminal groups may also be operating on behalf of their nation. Criminals who are either overtly or covertly funded by their country to commit cybercrime are termed nation state actors[5]. Persistently targeting individuals, organisations or countries, nation state actors, with the authority of or assistance from their country, seek to steal or destroy intellectual property or aim to compromise or disrupt private or public sector networks. Nation state actors may be involved in cyber espionage where they use technology and malware to spy on significant agencies or individuals and do so at the behest of, or to benefit, their country.

Hacktivists also use technology to compromise or disrupt agencies or individuals, but unlike nation state actors, they do this not for a national cause but for a social or political one. Hacktivists may deface websites, for example, to express their political dissent[6] or views on social issues. Hacktivists may also DDoS an agency or business that holds opposite views to their own to disrupt and garner attention to their cause. Other types of hacktivism may involve stealing restricted information and providing it to the public[7] in the view it is for the public good.

Organised criminal groups behind large cybercrime campaigns operate not unlike a legitimate business. These groups may use script kiddies to operate malware that has been developed by someone else in their group. Script kiddies also may be a part of other criminal enterprises or working on their own using the source code that has been developed by someone else. Nation state threat actors may perpetrate malicious cybercrime campaigns to disrupt, steal from or spy on their targets and do so for their country. Hacktivists may also target agencies, countries or business but they do this for their particular cause whether social or political. The diverse range of people behind cybercrime, as discussed in this chapter, are far removed from the stereotypical lone hacker of fiction.

## Key Takeaways

- Organised criminal groups may be behind large cybercrime campaigns and are nothing like the stereotypical lone hacker of fiction.
- Nation state actors commit cybercrime at the behest of, or with support from, their country.
- Hacktivists tend to commit cybercrime for a social or political cause.

## Chapter Sixteen

# CYBERCRIME - CHALLENGES FOR LAW ENFORCEMENT

".. the Internet knows no jurisdictional boundaries" – Jenny Ng[1]

To demystify the many elements of cybercrime, it is also important to understand the intrinsic challenges this crime type creates for law enforcement. While criminals who perpetrate cybercrime are not all stereotypical hackers in hoodies, the challenges law enforcement, intelligence agencies and judicial systems face in investigating, prosecuting or sanctioning cybercrime, does show that perpetrators can easily remain hidden. Cybercrime crosses continents and knows no geographical or jurisdictional boundaries making it very difficult for law enforcement to investigate or bring the criminals to justice. Another issue that is raised with cybercrime is how victims of scams are viewed.

Cybercrime is global, persistent and ever evolving making it challenging for policing and intelligence resources to keep up with.[2] Additionally, the complexities of technological crime[3] and time delays for international cooperation add more challenges to investigating perpetrators of cybercrime. Although in recent years there have been improvements in international cybercrime policing mutual assistance there are still many time delays and challenges involved. Cybercrime encompasses a massive amount of different crime types, including data, financial and identity theft, child exploitation and, when thinking of crimes against technology, disruption and sabotage. Cybercrime can also technologically evolve at a faster rate than law enforcement is trained, or has the tools, to deal with, as criminals keep adapting[4] to avoid detection. All of this increases the challenges for law enforcement as cybercrime can encompass many different forms of crime, keeps changing and, requires a variety of investigative and technological capabilities.

Another challenge for law enforcement when investigating cybercrime, is the inherent anonymity of committing crime via cyberspace rather than the physical world. With criminals using anonymising technology, such as the TOR browser[5] which is free, open-source software for anonymous internet communication, it is difficult to track the origin of the malware, email scam or criminal.

Of course it isn't just technology that makes cybercrime difficult for law enforcement, for example victims of romance or 419 scams may feel too embarrassed or insufficiently supported to report the crime or pursue a case. Particularly as defrauded victims may fear they will be blamed[6] for being scammed. Locating the scammers also can be very difficult as can gaining quick cross jurisdictional cooperation when they are found.

Crimes against or enabled by technology are many and varied and include crimes such as tech support scams, child exploitation, phishing, ransomware, data theft, DDOS and romance scams. With such diversity in technological crime police in the twenty-first century have massive challenges that their earlier counterparts did not.

## Key Takeaways

- Cybercrime crosses nations and policing jurisdictions which creates challenges for law enforcement.
- Criminals using anonymising browsers make it difficult for law enforcement to track the origin of the malware, email scam or criminal.
- With such a wide variety of cybercrime types, law enforcement in the twenty-first century have massive challenges that their earlier counterparts did not.
- The anonymity afforded by the internet creates extra challenges for law enforcement investigating crimes.

*Part Five*

# CYBER SECURITY

Often seen as something only the most computer literate or technical can understand, cyber security is important for all users of technology. Also known as Computer Security, Information Technology (IT) Security and Information Communications Technology (ICT) Security, cyber security encompasses everything about keeping our technology and communications secure and safe.

Just as we understand we need to lock our doors to mitigate against physical intrusion, we also all need to understand how to implement basic security measures to help protect us and our computers from cybercrime. This section provides an overview of cybersecurity, looks at some technology used to keep networks secure, explains exploits and vulnerabilities and, provides a look at some cybersecurity roles.

Cybersecurity basics need to be accessible and

understandable to all users of technology to help mitigate against cybercrime. With the ever evolving technological advances and an increased reliance on internet communications, cyber security is fast becoming the responsibility of everyone.

*Chapter Seventeen*

## WHAT IS CYBERSECURITY?

"A cybersecurity culture must be promoted at an international, national, organizational, and individual level to aid in minimizing risks from a human perspective in cyberspace. To promote such a culture it has to be understood and quantified in order to direct change. " - Adéle Da Veiga[1]

To help individuals and businesses better protect themselves from cybercrime, all users of technology need to adopt a stronger cyber security culture. This is easier said than done however, as so much of the cyber security world is tailored only to those with technology expertise. The aim of cyber security is to protect devices and networks from malicious attack and it is important for all users of technology to have at least a basic understanding of how to do this to protect themselves in cyberspace. Just as locking our doors before we leave home each day is part of our physical security culture, and not just the role of the locksmiths, so cyber security should be part of every day life for everyone using technology.

Cyber security is an umbrella term that includes things such as network, application, endpoint, data, cloud and mobile security as well as identity management, data governance, intelligence gathering, disaster recover and end user education. A major challenge in maintaining cyber security is keeping up with the ever evolving technology and criminal campaigns, this is one of the reasons why cyber security is such a diverse discipline.

Network security refers to the procedures, policies and tools used to help secure a computer network from criminal intrusion and compromise. To help keep networks secure requires a variety of tools and expertise to, check infrastructure for vulnerabilities, ensure firewalls are correctly configured and, monitor for intrusion. Application security is similar but focuses on the security of software rather than networks. Application security involves monitoring software for exploitable vulnerabilities and bugs and repairing or mitigating these.

Identity management in very basic terms relates to an account's user identity (ID), what access it has and what it can log into. If you use email or social media you will have an account that uses identity management to recognise you as the account holder. Using the correct authentication, such as a password or personal identification number (PIN), with the user ID provides access to the account or file. Authentication lets the identity in to the system and authorisation is what that identity can do once it gets in.

Cybersecurity is not the responsibility of one person, team or organisation, as all users of technology are responsible for contributing to security. As individuals we can all contribute to cybersecurity whether at home school or work. A strong cybersecurity culture is one that is with us all the time regardless of where we are. For businesses and individuals important and basic cybersecurity mechanisms are: keeping software and systems patched, using reputable and up-to-date antivirus applications, being cautious with public Wi-Fi, using strong passwords, using multi-factor authentication wherever possible and, keeping aware of scams and other cybercrime campaigns. These are not difficult to do and can be easily incorporated into the cybersecurity culture of all technology users.

The aim of cybersecurity is to help protect networks and information from compromise and other malicious attack. The concept of cybersecurity needs to be as normal to everyone as locking our doors when we leave the house. To help protect against cybercrime all users of technology need to adopt a strong cyber security culture to protect businesses, individuals and communities.

## Key Takeaways

- Cybersecurity is about keeping our

technology and communications secure and safe.
- Cybersecurity is a diverse discipline and needs to keep up with advances in technology.
- Cybersecurity is the responsibility of all users of technology.
- All users of technology need to adopt a strong cybersecurity culture.

## Chapter Eighteen
# TECHNOLOGY FOR CYBERSECURITY

---

"Meeting security responsibilities and providing for the confidentiality, integrity, and availability of information in today's highly networked environment can be a difficult task" – Toth and Klein[1]

---

There is no single solution that can be guaranteed to always protect people and networks from cybercrime. This is why there needs to be a wholistic approach to cybersecurity combining a strong cybersecurity culture, up to date cybercrime awareness and appropriately configured and patched systems and tools. Technology, in combination with other measures, can be used to support individuals and businesses to stay safer from cybercrime. This chapter looks at some commonly used technology that supports cyber security for individuals and businesses.

Anyone that uses emails will know the annoyance of spam and scam emails. This is where spam filters come in to help mitigate against these nuisance and often malicious emails. Many email clients have spam filters incorporated in them and commercial organisations may also add their own spam filtering solutions into their email gateways. There are a variety of types of spam filters that all work differently to help protect email inboxes from junk email, however all of them use a set of rules to work out whether an email is spam and needs to be redirected to the junk file.

Spam filters are not a total barrier to phishing emails but they are a way to help mitigate some of this malicious spam. Email spam filters can use a variety of ways to filter out spam, for example they may be content filters, rules-based filters, blacklist filters, header filters, permission filters, or challenge filters. Content filters check over the message in the email to cross reference with known spam words to decide if an email is spam. The filters that are rules-based have defined standards in which to check specific senders, subject lines or content, and black-list filters block emails coming in from known spam email addresses or domains. Email filters that search in the data sent in the headers, which contains all the information about the email and sender computer such as time stamps and sender IP address are call header filters. Permission filters only allow emails to be received by pre-approved senders and sender domains and challenge filters have a requirement that a sender must enter a specific code to be able to send the email.

To help keep computers safe from malware, it is also important to use a reliable and up to date anti-virus programme. The reason anti-virus solutions need to be kept up to date is that they can only scan and monitor computers for malware signatures that they know about. Malware signatures are the unique values that the malicious programmes have, like a fingerprint, and once an antivirus application knows that those values belong to a malicious application they can identify it. If the anti-virus software is not kept current it cannot update itself with what is known about new malware threats and therefore it will be unable to recognise and stop newer malware from infecting devices.

Firewalls are either hardware or software appliances that are configured to allow or deny traffic through a network. Traffic, in this sense, refers to data being transmitted from or to a network. For example, in what is called black listing, a firewall is configured by default to allow all traffic but to block known hostile traffic. The opposite of this is white listing where a firewall is configured to block all data communications by default with exceptions to allow traffic in and out only from known trusted entities.

There is no single solution to cybercrime protection, however there is a variety of technology both hardware and software that can help to protect from cybercrime campaigns and compromises.

## Key Takeaways

- There is no one single type of technical solution that can be guaranteed to always protect people from cybercrime.
- There needs to be a wholistic approach to cybersecurity
- Spam filters are not a total barrier to phishing emails however they are a way to help mitigate some of these malicious spam emails.
- To help keep computers safe from malware, it is important to use a reliable and up to date anti-virus programme.

## Chapter Nineteen
# CYBERSECURITY - VULNERABILITIES

---

"Vulnerabilities in a particular (online) environment could potentially be exploited by criminals and actors" - Choo[1]

---

Weaknesses in computer programming, networks, procedures or policies, that can be exploited by criminals, are known as security vulnerabilities. Vulnerabilities in networks or code can be exploited by criminals to gain access to restricted systems. The reason why software companies release security patches is to fix or mitigate security flaws that have been discovered in their code. White hat hackers, also known as pen testers, are employed to check for vulnerabilities in systems, and black hat hackers exploit them for their own malicious reasons. Vulnerabilities are reported on and recorded in the Common Vulnerabilities and Exposures (CVE) register which is a public domain database currently maintained by the not-for-profit MITRE corporation[2].

An application or hardware vulnerability that is not widely known about, except by the criminals exploiting it, and where there is yet no known fix, is called a zero-day exploit. Once the vulnerability becomes known and patches and other mitigations are implemented it is no longer a zero day. Until the zero-day exploit is patched or mitigated, it can be used by criminals to gain access to networks, applications or computers.

An example of an exploitable vulnerability, impacting certain Microsoft systems, was discovered in May 2019. The vulnerability was named BlueKeep and a criminal could exploit it to send malware to any unpatched Windows systems with remote desktop protocol enabled. Although Microsoft was quick to provide a patch, it still required people to implement it. In November 2019 a large-scale cybercrime campaign was discovered exploiting BlueKeep for cryptojacking[3]. Cryptojacking in simple terms involves transactions, without the knowledge or authority of the computer owner, to obtain virtual authority.

The first publicly known cryptojacking code was Coinhive[4], which was originally created for legitimate use, so that website owners could monetise their platforms in an alternative to selling advertising space. The code however was also used by criminals exploiting vulnerabilities in websites to embed the Coinhive code without the owners' knowledge or permission. Another cryptojacking code, called Bird Miner, was aimed at the MacOS and it stealthily stopped working whenever the activity monitor was run so the computer user remained unaware of the cryptojacking. These exploits used computer power to mine for crypto currency however they were not known to steal sensitive data.

Two major vulnerabilities, that when exploited allowed data to be stolen, became public in early 2018. Known as Meltdown and Spectre, the vulnerabilities were discovered in processors, also called central processing units (CPU), in a variety of computers. Meltdown[5] allowed applications to access system memory, whereas, Spectre[6] worked by tricking other applications into accessing memory. As these hardware vulnerabilities impacted nearly all computers regardless of operating system they were considered catastrophic[7].

Criminals can exploit vulnerabilities in applications and use these to steal passwords, gain access to networks and install malware. Companies, once a vulnerability is discovered, usually provide information and patches, for individuals and businesses to update their software to make it more secure. Monitoring and patching for vulnerabilities is not just the responsibility of large businesses and cybersecurity teams, as all users of technology need to ensure they keep their systems and software current and patched.

ey Takeaways

- Vulnerabilities in networks or code can be exploited by criminals to gain access to restricted systems.

- Software companies release security patches is to fix or mitigate security flaws.
- A vulnerability that is not widely known about, except by the criminals exploiting it, and where there is yet no known fix, is called a zero-day exploit.
- All users of technology need to ensure they keep their systems and software current and patched.

## Chapter Twenty
# CAREERS IN CYBER SECURITY

"Cloud computing and cybersecurity are only two areas that are expected to lead employment increases in the computer systems design and related services industry" - Lauren Csorny[1]

With cyberspace so popular with criminals, there is an increased need for cybersecurity professionals to help protect from and investigate cybercrime. The cybersecurity industry has diverse requirements and requires a wide variety of skills to support its aims. To demonstrate the diversity of roles in the industry, cybersecurity jobs include Chief Information Security Officers (CISO), analysts, risk assessors, software engineers, security architects, investigators, law enforcement, incident responders, intelligence officers, penetration testers and technical writers, to name just a few. This chapter provides a brief overview of a small amount of the many roles in cybersecurity.

## CISO AND CIO

Senior Executive level cybersecurity roles include CISO and Chief Information Officers (CIO). The CISO role dates back to the early 1990s when CitiBank suffered a large financial fraud attempt and realised it needed an official to oversee the bank's cyber security. As a result CitiBank appointed Steve Katz as the world's first CISO[2] in 1994. A CISO is a senior executive responsible for overseeing all of the cyber and information security strategies and policies of an organisation. A CIO overseas the technology strategies of an organisation and in some businesses may also have a similar role to the CISO.

## ANALYST

There are a variety of analyst roles in cybersecurity, such as cybercrime intelligence analyst, threat analyst, forensic analyst and incident response analyst. Analysts may be required to investigate cybersecurity incidents, monitor networks and email transmissions, analyse malware and, gather intelligence or evidence from a variety of sources. An analyst function in cybersecurity may exist in different teams such as law enforcement, intelligence agencies, Cyber Security Operations Centres (CSOC), Incident Response Teams and Threat Intelligence teams.

## RISK ASSESSESOR

Those involved in cybersecurity risk assessments identify everything an organisation has, including hardware, software, people, processes, policy and information, check how these may be impacted by a cybersecurity incident, and determine controls to manage the identified risks. Those involved in cyber security risk assessments also monitor and review the risks and mitigations at regular intervals. To ensure consistency in risk assessments, the International Organization for Standardization (ISO)[3], an independent internal body, provides framework and guidelines documents. For example, the international standard ISO 27005 provides information on how to conduct risk assessments and this standard complements ISO 27001[4], which provides a risk framework for information security management systems.

## SOFTWARE SECURITY ENGINEER

Software security engineers are responsible for ensuring software is secure which includes testing, debugging and monitoring software. The software security engineer may also be required to code solutions to security issues themselves. The role includes threat intelligence, identifying vulnerabilities and liaising with vendors to source effective security solutions.

## PENETRATION TESTER

A Penetration (pen) tester may also be termed a white hat hacker, as the role includes assessing vulnerabilities, in networks, people or policies, of an organisation to see what a criminal may be able to exploit. Pen testers may also assess web applications for exploitable vulnerabilities[5], about which they would then provide a report including recommendations for improvements. This role may be internal to the organisation or a business may hire a pen testing company to provide work on a contract basis.

## CYBERSECURITY TECHNICAL WRITER

The technical writer is required to create quality documentation on procedures, software and security assessments. They may have to liaise with other areas of a business and prepare documentation for risk audits and training.

## SUMMARY

Cybersecurity positions include analysts, pen testers, law enforcement, writers, risk assessors and senior management, all with a variety of skill types and expertise. The examples in this chapter of different cybersecurity roles provided just a glimpse into the diverse skill sets needed in this field. As technology continues to advance and as criminals continue to abuse it, there is an increasing need for a wide variety of cybersecurity professionals to help keep both individuals and businesses safer in cyberspace.

## Key Takeaways

- There is an increased need for cybersecurity professionals to help protect against and investigate cybercrime.
- The CISO role was created in 1994 by CitiBank and Steve Katz was the world's first CISO.
- Roles in cybersecurity are many and cover a variety of disciplines.
- As technology advances criminals find new ways to exploit it.

## Part Six
# DEMYSTIFY AND MITIGATE

The aim of this entire book is to help demystify cybercrime and make cyber security familiar, understandable and accessible to all people regardless of their experience with or knowledge of technology. The preceding chapters helped to provide some foundation information about the history of computing and hacking, then gave a brief overview of malware and scams. The previous section dealt with the many ways technology can be used to commit crimes such as child exploitation and, looked at data breaches and privacy. The previous chapter provided a very brief overview of some of the reasons policing cybercrime is challenging, which was included to help encourage an understanding of the difficulties law enforcement face with cybercrime. This section brings all of the previous chapters together, briefly explains the history of the Internet and, focuses on different mechanisms people can use to help protect themselves from cybercrime.

Cybersecurity and cybercrime awareness are important for everyone as we live in an ever-interconnected age where technology is all around us. Demystifying cybercrime and showing that hackers are not all evil genius shadowy figures typing code to access networks helps to normalise cyber security, make it less mysterious and make it more accessible for all users of technology. Let's make cyberspace a safe place for all people and not the playground of criminals!

## Chapter Twenty-One
# A BRIEF HISTORY OF COMPUTERS

---

"Few figures in the long history of computing generate more passion and sometimes more enmity than Charles Babbage and Ada Lovelace." - Thomas Misa[1]

---

The concept of demystifying cybercrime and unmasking the hacker, is not just about ensuring users of technology understand and have an increased awareness of cybercrime and security. It is also relevant to look briefly at the history of computing itself, not just cybercrime, to gain a better understanding of the technology either being used for crime or being made more secure from it. An understanding of some of the early history of computing can help to provide a foundation of the technology we use and how it can be used by criminals. Additionally, while there exists a stereotype of males being the ones behind advances in computing, there are also many women in history who played significant roles in creating and developing the technology as we know it today.

Going back to the early 1800s, Joseph Jacquard, developed his programmable punch card automated looms. This automated technology that programmed designs into the woven fabric, also had a type of card reader that would insert the next punch card into place every time the shuttle took thread through. Also in the 1800s, a mathematician, engineer and inventor, called Charles Babbage invented a calculating machine he named the Difference Engine. The Difference Engine was an automated mechanical calculator and, although not programmable, it was a precursor to the modern computation devices. By the mid 1830s Babbage started designs on what he called the Analytical Engine. The Analytical Engine was designed to use the punch card instruction input as per the looms that Jacquard created. Unfortunately, due to limitations at the time, the Analytical Engine was never completed.

It is thought that a demonstration of Charles Babbage's Difference Engine[2] to a teenaged Ada Lovelace that may have inspired her interest in mathematics and inspired her to become another pioneer of modern computing. Augusta Ada King the Countess of Lovelace was the child of the poet Lord Byron and the mathematician Baroness Byron. Ada was a polymath from a young age with a variety of eclectic interests and the work of Babbage and his Analytical Engine interested her as a mathematician. She translated a book about his work, the "Sketch of the Analytical

Engine" written by Menabrea[3], and also added her own ideas and descriptions into a reference manual. In the book she articulated that Babbage's invention was far more than a calculating machine. Lovelace was intrigued by Babbage's Analytical Engine designs, and the fact it was programmable via instructions input with punch cards, becoming the foremost expert on the use of punch cards to programme calculating devices. Because of her understanding of programming with punch cards, Ada Lovelace is sometimes considered the first computer programmer.

In the mid 1930s, the Z1[4], considered to be the first functional modern type of computer[5], was created by Konrad Zuse. The computer was coded via punch cards, made out of celluloid film, similar to the punch card concept used in both Jacquard's looms and the Babbage Analytical Engine in the nineteenth century. The Z1 was thought to weigh at least 1000kg, was not portable and could not easily be mass produced.

While the Z1 may have been the first functional modern computer, the first electrically programmable one is considered to be the Colossus[6]. A large, programmable, decoding machine, the Colossus was developed in Britain to support the Military Intelligence code breakers[7]. The United States also developed a computer, to support war efforts, it was called the Electronic Numerical Integrator and Computer (ENIAC).

ENIAC is thought to be the first completely electronic digital computing device. In the 1940s, Jean Bartik was one of six main programmers for ENIAC, the others being Elizabeth (Betty) Holberton, with whom she was co-programming lead, Frances Spence,

Marlyn Melzer, Ruth Teitelbaum and Kathleen McNulty. In 1948, Jean Bartik was instrumental in converting the ENIAC technology into one that could store programming[8] making it more efficient and quicker to calculate. After World War II, Bartik worked with the ENIAC creators to develop the computing machines called the Binary Automatic Computer (BINAC) and the Universal Automated Computer (UNIVAC). The first computer to use magnetic tape instead of punch cards, BINAC was also the first to have a user manual.

While computing technology was being invented to support military efforts, so were ways to transmit secure communications. In 1942 for example, actor Hedy LaMarr[9], in collaboration with George Antheil, developed and patented a secret transmissions technology. Her invention is considered to be the foundation for the modern Wi Fi, Bluetooth and GPS technology.

After World War II, developments in computing continued, however it wasn't until the 1950s, that computers were mass produced. In 1953 IBM introduced the mass produced 701[10], developed for military purposes[11], that was capable of 2200 computations per second. These computers were still far too bulky and large for personal use, but in the 1970s the first personal computers were developed. Although the KENBAK-1 micro-computer was introduced in 1971, the term personal computer was thought to have been coined by Ed Roberts[12] with his ALTAIR 8800 in 1975. The ALTAIR 8800 was sold in both kit form and ready assembled. A year later, Steve Jobs and Steve Wozniak[13] developed their Apple I [14]kit computer and in 1977 they released the pre-assembled Apple II.

This chapter provided a very brief look at some of the historical advances in computing. The 1800s saw Jacquard's punch card loom, Babbage's analytical engine and Ada Lovelace's coding. In the mid 1930s the first modern type of functional computer was created that used punched celluloid for programming. The advent of World War II brought with it a need to advance technology to support the military, so Britain created the Colossus and the United States had the ENIAC. Although the first mass produced computer was launched in 1953, it wasn't until the 1970s that computers started to become smaller and their popularity increased for both business and individual users.

**Key Takeaways**

- Women played a significant role in the development of the computer and programming.
- The Binary Automatic Computer was the first to use magnetic tape and the first to have a user manual.
- Large computing devices were developed in World War II to support decryption of coded messages.
- IBM developed the first mass produced computer and Ed Roberts created the first personal computer.

## Chapter Twenty-Two

# THE WORLD OF THE WEB

"The Web as I envisaged it, we have not seen it yet. The future is still so much bigger than the past." – Sir Tim Berners-Lee[1]

Cybercrime, hackers and the dark web are often terms used together and, the idea of a part of the Internet that is used for criminal activities by these shadowy hackers sounds both horrifying and mysterious. The Internet brings information from all over the world, crossing geographical boundaries, to the computers of individuals and businesses, and it also used to commit crimes and drop malware. To help demystify cybercrime it helps to include a basic explanation of the Internet, including a brief history of the world wide web and then look at the differences between the dark, deep and surface web.

Although the terms are sometimes used interchangeably, the Internet and the world wide web are not the same thing. The Internet is the structure in which the world wide web communication and retrieval framework exists. The Internet dates back to at least fifty years with the Advanced Research Projects Agency Network (ARPANET)[2] when the United States Defense Advanced Research Projects Agency (DARPA) researched ways for computers to communicate with each other[3]. The research was referred to as the Internetting project which gradually evolved into the term Internet. Over the years the researchers developed a way for the computers to transmit data via linked packet systems with the transmission control protocol (TCP) and the Internet protocol (IP).

The concept of the world wide web was proposed in 1989 by Sir Tim Berners-Lee to establish a more efficient way to share information between researchers and universities. By 1990, he and his colleagues at CERN had developed a better way for the Internet to be navigated, with the Hyper Text Markup Language (HTML) that created a standardised Internet communication framework. The use of hypertext links, also known as hyperlinks, however, dates back much further to the 1960s. The online system, that used hypertext links, was known by the acronym NLS and was created by Douglas Englebert and implemented by the Augmentation Research Centre (ARC)[4]. As an aside this system was also known for its windowed screens and the use of a mouse. Hyper Text Transfer Protocol (HTTP), also developed at

CERN in work initiated by Berners-Lee, is the framework in which computers transmit and receive information over the Internet. The first iteration of this protocol had one method, called GET, to obtain a web page.

By 1991, the World Wide Web was open for anyone to use and was, as we know, later keenly adopted. In 1993 the first web browser that displayed both images and text was created. This browser was called Mosaic and it had the point and click navigation similar to how browsers are used today. The release of this browser helped to gain increased adoption of the world wide web by more people. A more secure extension of the HTTP, called HTTPS, was created in 1994 by the company called Netscape. This encrypted transfer protocol was initially created to support the need for more secure credit cards transactions.

In terms of the modern Internet, there are three layers of the world wide web, known as surface, deep and dark web. The surface web, also called indexed or visible, describes all of the content that has been indexed and can be discovered publicly via search engines. The surface web is a small proportion of all of the world wide web; however, it is the part most people know and use. The deep web describes the remainder of the web and it is estimated to be at least five hundred[5] times larger than the surface web. The deep web contains all the non-indexed pages and is not discoverable via search engines. The deep web can include archived pages, private business databases, business intranets, webmail platforms, databases, banking platforms and other web sites that have services that require credentialing to access.

Within the deep or non-indexed web, there is a

small part in an anonymous network, the darkweb or darknet, that can only be accessed via a specific browser, called TOR. This browser took its name from a project called the Onion Router (TOR), an anonymised open source browser developed in the mid 1990s at the United States Naval Research Lab (NRL) by David Goldschlag, Mike Reed, and Paul Syverson[6]. The browser is devised to encrypt and move the network traffic via many different servers to make it difficult to trace back. The TOR browser is a legitimate application and in of itself is not malicious. In fact the Tor Project, that started with the work at the NRL, was originally aimed at people who want to stop their web habits being used to target them for advertising, those who wish to remain private such as government agencies and also those wishing to avoid censorship such as journalists[7]. The dark web is a place for criminals to sell malware, child exploitation material and other criminal endeavours, however it is also used for legitimate reasons that require extra privacy and secrecy.

Two online criminal marketplaces, Silk Road and Alpha Bay[8], names which became public after they were shut down, both operated on the dark web. The first of the main dark web online marketplaces, Silk Road, only accessible via the TOR browser, was known for the sale of illegal drugs and other illicit commodities.

The Internet is the name of the massive international network infrastructure on which the World Wide Web sits. The World Wide Web has three layers, the surface web, the deep web and the dark web. The deep and dark web are parts of the internet that are not indexed by search engines. Not all of the dark web is used by criminals although due to its hidden nature it provides an ideal environment for illicit activities.

##  Key Takeaways

- The Internet and the world wide web are not the same thing. The Internet is the structure in which the world wide web communication and retrieval framework exists.
- The concept of the world wide web was proposed in 1989 by Sir Tim Berners-Lee to establish a more efficient way to share information between researchers and universities.
- In terms of the modern Internet, there are three layers of the world wide web, known as surface, deep and dark web.

## Chapter Twenty-Three
## PROTECTION FROM CYBERCRIME

"... increasingly, cyber and privacy professionals are seeking ways to educate the community, our governments and organizations about how to protect themselves from cybercrime." – Nicole Stephensen [1]

Demystifying cybercrime is necessary to support understanding on how we can all protect ourselves from the many cyber enabled scams and crimes against technology out in the world. The more we understand cybercrime the better we can protect ourselves and educate others to ensure they are aware this crime type and can pursue means to protect themselves against it too. Cybercrime is not committed by stereotypical hoody wearing super technical and mysterious evil genius types, it is committed by criminals. Victims of cybercrime are not to blame for what has happened to them[2]; the criminal is! Just as locking your house's front door to help protect against burglars is not mysterious, so should the basic techniques to help people mitigate against cybercrime be as common. There is no 100% solution to protect against cybercrime, but then locking doors is not a total guarantee against house break and enter either, but locking doors makes it harder for criminals to get in. Just as in physical security, there is no one complete solution to protecting against cybercrime, but instead there are layers of security measures that can be implemented to support people to protect themselves from cybercrime. Cyber security is everyone's business, so this chapter looks at some basic measures we can all take to protect ourselves from cybercrime.

As phishing emails tend to be a main way for criminals to compromise accounts, steal money and information and introduce malware into their targets' computers, it pays to understand simple ways to help protect ourselves from this type of scam. When an email is spoofed, the display name and actual email address are different, so take care to check that the display name matches the sender's email address. If there are hyperlinks in an email, hover over them with the mouse but do not click, when you hover over the link, have a look at what the actual link is. Take a moment to think about what the email says, check that it is written in the usual way that individual or company writes when you receive email from them. Be wary when an email subject line or message body contains urgent or threatening language, consider if this is the way the company or person would normally address you or the situation. If an email contains an attachment, consider whether or not you were expecting one form the sender or if the attachment is something you would normally receive. If an email requests money to be transferred or sensitive information to be provided check with the purported sender via other means before actioning the request to verify the email is legitimate. While spam filters, email gateways and anti-virus applications provide some layers of security, it is important to not allow a false sense of security in them or your own abilities in spotting a scam. Just because your company, or even you as an individual, may be using the best spam filters and other security software, does not means you will not receive a malicious email.

An old saying of 'if it looks too good to be true it probably is' applies very well to cybercrime. For example, websites, emails and social media posts, that share unbelievable specials or huge discounts on usually very expensive or luxury items, may be scams. Always check website addresses before following links shared on social media or emails to be sure you end up on the legitimate website. Better still, locate the web site from a search engine and access it via a browser bypassing the shared link. When shopping online look for the 'HTTPS' on retail web sites as these sites are security certificated. Beware however that some criminals do purchase security certificates to create HTTPS websites, so this alone is not proof of legitimacy! While shopping online, also be very cautious about providing financial information such as credit cards on unsecured sites, look for ones that have secure connections and encryption of personal data or use a trusted and reliable third-party site to transfer money.

Shopping online also means home delivery and postal pick up, two services that are often spoofed in phishing emails. Be wary of emailed delivery confirmations, particularly if you were not expecting anything to be delivered. It is often advisable to err on the side of caution and not click the links in these even if you are expecting a delivery. Check who the sender is, or says they are, is that the postal service or shop you were expecting an email from? Hover over the link first to see what the actual website address is, and better still go to the legitimate business website by searching for it or entering the known website address manually to get the tracking updates and details. There are known phishing scams where the emails spoof major postal or delivery companies, the attachments may contain trojans such as emotet, or the emails may have links taking the potential victim to a phishing website where account credentials or financial information may be stolen after keyed in by the user.

Being safer from cybercrime doesn't just mean understanding how cyber enabled scams and malware work, there are other types of cybercrime that can steal financial or other credentials and personal information. For example, beware of free Wi-Fi as a connection that may appear to be legitimate. as provided by a shop or public facility, may actually be one run by scammers. Criminals can create open Wi-Fi names that look like ones that are expected in that location, for example in a motel the legitimate Wi-Fi may appear as Free_-Motel_WiFI, and the criminals may create their own called Motel_Free_WiFi. Even legitimately provided free Wi-Fi may lack appropriate encryption and leave your banking or other restricted account details and credentials available for criminals to steal.

## HINTS FOR SAFER USE OF TECHNOLOGY

The intention of this book is to demystify cybercrime and make cyber security more accessible, understandable and attainable for all users of technology. If only one part of this book is read, please make it this section about hints for using technology in a safer way!

### SEASONAL SCAMS

Any significant retail event or seasonal holiday makes for great cybercrime attempts!

While people are looking forward to seasonal holidays, buying gifts and getting bargains, criminals are looking forward to exploiting them. Looking for online bargains? Please check the spelling of the link you are on as criminals buy and register web domains with common typos of well-known stores. Just to trick shoppers and steal their PII and money.

So many successful seasonal sales on legitimate websites, leads to criminals creating faked retailer pages to trick shoppers into sharing their money and details with them. Criminals are known to buy website domain names that are typos of legitimate sites and also to buy certificates to ensure the website is 'HTTPS' making it appear legitimate. For example, say that a major retailer has a site called 'https happysales com' a criminal may purchase a site with security certification and words that look similar, 'https happysaIes com'. The criminals may even send spam emails spoofing well known retailers and direct people to their faked retail sites where they phish for credit card details and personal information. When taking advantage of seasonal sales and bargains don't let criminals take advantage of you!

- Check website addresses before you enter any details, is it the legitimate site for that retailer?
- Only enter financial information on secured connections and also do not enter any personal or financial details while on free WiFi.
- Do not provide more information than needed. Do they really need your full birth date to sell you a magazine subscription?
- Be wary of discounts that sound too good to be true – because they probably are!

## SCAM EMAILS

With email being commonly used by so many, and not just for work, it is no surprise it is also used by people to commit crime. Emails spoofing businesses such as postal and telecommunications services, government agencies and software companies may be sent by criminals in phishing campaigns to gain unauthorised access to retail and software account log in details and financial information. In business email compromise scams, for example, criminals may send emails that spoof senior employees, or even send from compromised business accounts, to trick people into paying faked invoices or to send regular payments to a different bank account. While there are software applications that can block emails that appear suspicious, they are not a complete mitigation to these scams. It is important that any user of emails stays aware of how to check if an email looks like a scam.

- Check the display name against the email address.
- If on a computer, hover over and check links with your mouse pointer (do NOT click on the links to see where they go), does the link look as expected for that company?
- Analyse the salutation and sentence style, is this how the sender would be expected to write?
- Beware of urgent or threatening language in the subject line.
- Be cautious of attachments you weren't expecting.
- Don't offer to pay, change or provide information without verifying the sender's legitimacy.

## TECH SUPPORT SCAMS

Also known as remote access scams, the criminal aims to convince their potential target that their computer has malware and that they need to download remote access software so the computer can be fixed. These scams may be via cold calling, web site pop-ups or even via scam emails.

- Remember that telecommunications and computer companies do not proactively call people unsolicited to tell them there is malware on their computers.
- Do not give remote access of your computer to anyone unless you can confirm the request is legitimate and from a genuine technical support company that you do business with.
- Do not believe pop-ups that state your computer has malware and suggest you call a number or download and run software to repair it.
- If you have already been scammed delete any software they asked you to install, change your passwords, call your financial institutions to cancel any credit card that may have been provided to the scammer and to attempt to claim back any money that has been scammed.

## PROTECTING FROM THE IMPACT OF RANSOMWARE

Whether a business or an individual, ransomware can cause loss of saved information and software as well as major disruption. While there are technological ways to help prevent ransomware attacks, like all cybercrime these are not a guarantee. This is why it is necessary to take steps to protect yourself from ransomware.

- Change all default passwords that came with the routers, systems or software.
- Have spam filters in place whether in personal email clients or in business email gateways.
- Keep all software patched with current versions.
- Use a reputable anti-virus that is up to date.
- Keep current back ups on your data and software that are stored offline.
- If infected by ransomware, it is better NOT to pay the ransom. There is no guarantee you will get your data back even if you pay. By paying you will then also let the criminals know that you have funds that they may then try other ways to extort.

## BEING SAFER ONLINE

How to be safer online is a topic that could make an entire book in itself, however there are some basic steps that everyone can take to keep when using the internet.

- Use a reputable, up to date anti virus
- Keep the browser software up to date
- If the browser software has a pop-up blocker use it
- Do not reuse passwords
- Be cautious with free public Wi-Fi
- Do not click on links offering unbelievable impossible discounts and offers
- Be cautious with what you download, make

sure the application or file is from a legitimate source
- Do not overshare ion social media and be cautious about suspicious friend or connection requests from people you do not know

## SOCIAL MEDIA SECURITY TIPS

Social media, blogging and video sharing sites are increasing in popularity as a way to communicate with the world via the Internet. It is important to use these sites with safety and security in mind, as there is nothing private on the Internet!

- Do not share information online that could put you at risk of identity theft or physical threats.
- Be cautious of sharing photos online that identify your car, home address, or children's school.
- Check the privacy settings on the social media platform and adjust them as necessary.
- Limit work details online, do not post full resumes or all your work contact details on a public social media platform
- Verify the connection or friend request is from a genuine account and not a scammer or someone impersonating another.
- Consider how the social media site may use your personal information and be accordingly cautious.

- Use a strong password that you have not used elsewhere.
- Be cautious clicking on links shared on social media.
- If a post shares a discount, giveaway or offer that sounds too good to be true, it potentially is a scam.
- Log out of the social media account after each use.

## Key Takeaways

- Anyone can fall victim to cybercrime, remember that none of us are immune.
- Cybercrime is more than scams and malware, it also encompasses other cyber enabled criminal activities such as child exploitation.
- Stay aware and share your knowledge of cybercrime, malware, scams, and other cyber enabled criminal activity to support others to also be vigilant.
- The victims of cybercrime are not at fault, the criminals are. Let's change the narrative and stop victim blaming.
- Collaboration and awareness are key to hardening our communities against cybercrime.

## Chapter Twenty-Four
# UNMASKING THE HACKER

"Hackers are seen as shadowy figures with superhuman powers that threaten civilization."
– Mitch Kapor[1]

Why is the mysterious hacker in a hoody stereotype so prolific? How does the image of an ominous omnipotent being wearing a hoody, and skulking in front of a keyboard, help us to understand and protect ourselves from cybercrime? In short, it doesn't.

Let's change the narrative and make cybercrime less of a mystery and more easily understood by all users of technology. By doing this, cyber security becomes more accessible and a normal part of everyday life. The concept of unmasking the hacker includes understanding that hackers are a diverse cohort, not all criminals who commit cybercrime are hackers and, not all hackers are criminals.

Crimes against or enabled by technology are not new, and neither are they all the work of hackers. Hacking is about using exploits against technological vulnerabilities in networks or devices to gain access to them. Cyber enabled scams that gain credentials and thereby access to computer networks or systems are not hacking, they are scams. Since the advent of automation and technology there has been many variants of criminal activity targeting or using it to commit crimes. When Jacquard invented his punch card automated looms in the early 1800s, for example, his technology was targeted by activists who were concerned they would lose their jobs due to the automation. Hacking and intercepting communication signals dates back to at least 1903 with Maskelyne's compromise of Marconi's allegedly secure and private long-distance telegraph. These crimes were against or enabled by technology although the perpetrators were not hackers, they were criminals sabotaging equipment or compromising private telecommunication signals.

In the 1950s the term hacking was used by members of the MIT Tech Model Railroad Club and referred to their tinkering and experimenting first with the trains and signals and later with computers. There arose a golden age of hacking, where people tinkered with or hacked technology, and committed crimes that somehow appeared less about being malicious and more about experimenting, The phone phreaks, for example, started off out of fascination for the telephony and how they could obtain free long distance calls by tricking the phone networks with their own whistles and clicks. With the advent of the Internet and the popularity of computing devices, cybercrime started to impact more individuals and organisations in increasingly serious ways.

Social engineering, a way to psychologically manipulate a person, is used extensively to enable crime via or against computers. Phishing emails appeal to a variety of psychological triggers for success. For example, they use the names of well-known companies, or people known to the target, to be believable. Phishing emails appeal to the recipients emotions by promoting a sense of urgency in the subject line and message and, they appeal to a target's false sense of security that their email spam filters or anti-virus will stop malicious emails. People behind phishing scams are not necessarily shadowy figures writing code to exploit vulnerabilities and hacking into restricted networks, they are instead criminals exploiting human psychology. Malware is also not always written by the criminals using it, instead they may buy it ready to use from people who specialise in selling malware as a service.

As the world becomes increasingly interconnected and computing progresses, criminals and organised criminal associations continue to exploit technology to commit a variety of crimes. Understanding more about how cybercrime works can help to demystify it and help all users of technology to understand how to increase their cyber security and harden their communities against cybercrime. Demystifying cybercrime and unmasking the hacker to change the hoody-wearing elite hacker narrative is important as it makes cybercrime less of a mystery. This in turn makes protection from cybercrime more accessible. Both the non-technical and technical alike can increase their awareness of, and protection from cybercrime knowing it is not being perpetrated by super human hackers. Crimes against or enabled by technology are neither new nor mystical. We need to keep raising awareness of cybercrime, demystifying it and helping everyone understand how to be safer online.

The start of the twenty-first century saw the rise of black, grey and white hat hackers. The terms are a nod to old Western shows where the good character wore a white hat and the bad one a black, please note they are not talking about hoodies! Ethical hackers, also known as white hats, are hired to perform checks on the security of networks, grey hat hackers look for security flaws in networks but are not authorised to do so, whereas black hat hackers exploit vulnerabilities in networks for malicious intent. Additionally, black hat hackers with the expertise to create malicious code or find vulnerabilities in networks to exploit may sell their services to others. Not all of these hacker types are criminals and not all criminals committing cybercrime are hackers.

Lots of different malware code and campaigns exist, and many of these are distributed via scam emails. Email is also a mechanism that criminals use to steal account credentials from their victims by tricking them into providing their credentials on spoofed corporate web sites or by placing malware on the victim's computer that steals account information. Anyone can fall victim to cybercrime and there is no solely technical solution to prevent it. Phishing emails rely on being believable, playing to emotions and the false sense of security of the recipient. If you are ticked then later realise that you have entered your credentials on to a phishing site, change your password! Do not feel embarrassed as anyone can fall victim to cybercrime, nobody is immune. Check what the criminal may have had access to with those credentials, maybe you need to contact your bank or cancel a credit card. Anyone can fall victim to cybercrime, so have a plan of action in case you do. If you operate a business, have an appropriate incident response plan, if you are an individual think of what you would need to do should your credentials be stolen, or your computer encrypted with malware. Better still, have a plan of action to make it harder for you or your business to be impacted by cybercrime. If your computer is impacted by cybercrime be careful where you go to get it fixed. Take care not to be defrauded by tech support scams.

Tech support scammers, like those who send phishing, use social engineering to trick their victims. Scammers who pretend to be technical support representatives of major software or telecommunications companies, contact the potential victims via telephone or by using malvertising or website popups. Tech support scammers convince their victims into installing legitimate remote access software that they then use to access the victim's computer, pretend it has malware on it and request payment to fix it. While the criminals have access to the victim's computer, they may also install malware or steal account and banking credentials. Tech support scams are not perpetrated by mysterious shadowy figures but by criminals who use social engineering to defraud people. These scams are run by criminal business organisations, with managers, coaches, web developers, recruiters and telemarketers, all working hard to create just the right atmosphere to scam their victims.

By perpetuating the mysterious shadowy hacker narrative, non-technical users of technology may believe it is all too difficult to protect themselves against cybercrime. However, cyber security needs to be made accessible to everyone who uses technology regardless of their understanding of the computing devices or networks they use. There needs to be a shift from the elite hacker and elite technical person concept and move towards a realisation that cybercrime is just another crime type and, just like any other crime, there are things individuals and businesses can do to make the online world safer for themselves.

As long as there is crime and technology there will always be some form of cybercrime, and therefore there will always be some unfortunate individual or business that has fallen victim to it. Whose fault is this? It is the fault of the criminals behind the malware, scam, exploitation, trafficking, or whatever else they have perpetrated. It is not the victim's fault. We need to all work together to harden our communities as cybercrime targets. Let's all make it harder for any of us to be scammed, exploited, have our computers infected or participating in a DDoS as part of a BotNet. How do we do this? Let's start by collaborating, helping each other, sharing information and destroying the evil genius hacker narrative once and for all.

Cybercrime is neither new nor mystical and the concept of mysterious shadowy hackers in hoodies being behind all cybercrime incidents is more an imaginative construct of modern media and fiction than reality. Crimes against or enabled by technology are perpetrated by criminals and not all of them are hackers, additionally not all hackers are criminals. Like all criminal activities there are many reasons why cybercrime is committed, different people or groups perpetrating it and, many different crime types involved. Demystifying cybercrime and making it more understandable for non-technical users of technology, helps people understand better how they can protect themselves from this crime type.

The mysterious technical elite hacker narrative may make consumers of technology believe that cybercrime awareness and cyber security are highly technical issues that are inaccessible to the general public. This can create an obstacle to non-technical users of computers and the Internet and prevent them from learning about and applying cybercrime mitigations. Unmasking the hacker stereotype is about making cyber security accessible to all people, which is important as the world moves to a more technological and interconnected space.

**We need to stop the binary-curtained, hoody-wearing elite hacker narrative and reinforce that cybercrime is just another crime type that, although it causes challenges for law enforcement to police, is a crime we don't have to be technical to protect ourselves from.**

# WHERE TO GO FOR HELP

## AUSTRALIA

**ACSC** www.cyber.gov.au/
**Report cybercrime** www.cyber.gov.au/report
**Identity theft support** www.idcare.org
**Cyber safety information** www.staysmartonline.gov.au/
**Australian Privacy Commissioner** www.oaic.gov.au/
**Scam Watch** www.scamwatch.gov.au
**eSafety commissioner** www.esafety.gov.au
**Think U Know** www.thinkuknow.org.au
**AFP** www.afp.gov.au
**AusCERT** www.auscert.org.au
**Have I been Pwned** Haveibeenpwned.com

## USA

**US-CERT** www.us-cert.gov
**Report identity theft** identitytheft.gov
**Cyber safety information** www.dhs.gov/stop-thinkconnect

## UNITED KINGDOM

**NCSC** www.ncsc.gov.uk
**Report cybercrime** report.ncsc.gov.uk
**Cyber safety information** getsafeonline.org
**Information Commissioner's Office** ico.org.uk

## USEFUL LINKS - INTERNATIONAL

**Computer vulnerabilities and exposures (CVE) list** cve.mitre.org
**NIST cyber security** www.nist.gov/topics/cyber-security
**Krebs on Security** - https://krebsonsecurity.com/
**ISO** - www.iso.org

## PODCASTS

**Cyber Security Cafe** www.cybersecuritycafe.com.au
**Privacy Matters** iotsecurityinstitute.com/iotsec/index.php/privacy-matters-show
**Karissa Breen KBKasts** karissabreenindustries.com/kbkast/
**Risky Business** risky.biz/netcasts/risky-business
**Security Weekly** - securityweekly.com
**Darknet Diaries** - darknetdiaries.com
**Smashing Security** - www.smashingsecurity.com

# NOTES

## 1. THE FIRST HACKER?

1. Marks, P. (2011). The Edwardian hacker who embarrassed Marconi. *New Scientist*, *212*(2844), 48-49.
2. Appleby, J., Appleby, J. O., & Schlesinger Jr, A. M. (2003). *Thomas Jefferson: The American Presidents Series: The 3rd President, 1801-1809* (Vol. 3). Macmillan.
3. Roemer, E. (1960). Jean Louis Pons, Discoverer of Comets. *Leaflet of the As*
4. Fitzsimmons, M. P. (2010). *From Artisan to Worker: Guilds, the French State, and the Organization of Labor, 1776–1821*. Cambridge University Press.
5. Kurfess, T. R. (2004). *Robotics and automation handbook*. CRC press.
6. Sekgwathe, V., & Talib, M. (2012). Cyber forensics: Computer security and incident response. *International Journal of New Computer Architectures and Their Applications*, *2*(1), 127-138.
7. Corr, H. (2004). Agnes Dollan (1887-1966), suffragette and socialist.
8. Dauncey, H., & Hare, G. (2004). *The Tour de France, 1903-2003: a century of sporting structures, meanings and values*. Routledge.
9. Nassa, V. K. Wireless Communications: Past, Present and Future. *Dronacharya Research Journal*, *50*.
10. Hong, S. (2001). *Wireless: From Marconi's black-box to the audion*. MIT Press.
11. Gordon, S., & Ford, R. (2006). On the definition and classification of cybercrime. *Journal in Computer Virology*, *2*(1), 13-20.

## 2. GOLDEN AGE OF HACKING

1. Yagoda, Ben (2014) http://www.newyorker.com/tech/elements/a-short-history-of-hack
2. Satapathy, S., & Patra, R. R. (2015). Ethical Hacking. *International Journal of Scientific and Research Publications*, *5*(6).
3. Levy, S. (1984). *Hackers: Heroes of the computer revolution* (Vol. 14). Garden City, NY: Anchor Press/Doubleday.
4. Orth, M. (1971). For Whom Ma Bell Tolls Not. *Los Angeles Times*, *31*.
5. Becker, R. A., Volinsky, C., & Wilks, A. R. (2010). Fraud detection

in telecommunications: History and lessons learned. *Technometrics, 52*(1), 20-33.
6. Worsham, J. L. From Phone Phreaking to Cyber War: Cyber Crime's Impact on Business An Economic Impact Study for Risk Assessment.
7. Lapsley, P. (2013). Phreaking out ma bell. *IEEE Spectrum, 50*(2), 30-35.
8. Lapsely, P. (2013). The Definitive Story of Steve Wozniak, Steve Jobs, and Phone Phreaking. *The Atlantic (20 February 2013)*.
9. Lapsley, P. (2013). Exploding the phone: The untold story of the teenagers and outlaws who hacked Ma Bell. Grove Press
10. Johnson, L. (2010). COMPUTER CRACKING: The case of Kevin Mitnick. Forensic Examiner, 19(3), 22.
11. Fell, J. (2017). Cyber crime-History: Hacking through history. *Engineering & Technology, 12*(3), 30-31.
12. Mitnick, K. D., & Simon, W. L. (2009). *The Art of Intrusion: The real stories behind the exploits of hackers, intruders and deceivers*. John Wiley & Sons.
13. Bell, S., & Oudshoorn, M. (2018, October). Meeting the Demand: Building a Cybersecurity Degree Program With Limited Resources. In *2018 IEEE Frontiers in Education Conference (FIE)* (pp. 1-7). IEEE.
14. Qasim, N., & Rind, M. Q. TECHNIQUES USED FOR HACKING THE INFORMATION. *Islamic Countries Society of Statistical Sciences*, 441.
15. Furnell, S., & Spafford, E. H. (2019). The Morris Worm at 30. *ITNOW, 61*(1), 32-33.
16. Noll, S. (2019). Patient Zero and the Making of the AIDS Epide
17. Al Hajri, H. H., Al Mughairi, B. M., Karim, A. M., Nasiruzzaman, M., & Hossain, M. I. (2019). Ransomware a Concealed Weapon of Cyber Extortion: The Beginning Unfolded. *INTERNATIONAL JOURNAL OF ACADEMIC RESEARCH IN BUSINESS AND SOCIAL SCIENCES, 9*(7).

## 3. END OF THE 20TH CENTURY AND Y2K

1. Best, K. (2003). Revisiting the Y2K bug: Language wars over networking the global order. *Television & New Media, 4*(3), 297-319.
2. Quiggin, J. (2005). The Y2K scare: causes, costs and cures. *Australian Journal of Public Administration, 64*(3), 46-55.
3. Best, K. (2003). Revisiting the Y2K bug: Language wars over networking the global order. *Television & New Media, 4*(3), 297-319.
4. Lindup, K. (1995). The arrest of Kevin Mitnick. *Network Security, 3*(1995), 16-19.
5. Rader, M., & Rahman, S. (2015). Exploring historical and emerging

phishing techniques and mitigating the associated security risks. *arXiv preprint arXiv:1512.00082*.
6. Knapp, K. J., & Boulton, W. R. (2007). Ten information warfare trends. In *Cyber Warfare and Cyber Terrorism* (pp. 17-25). IGI Global.
7. Garber, L. (1999). Melissa virus creates a new type of threat. *Computer*, (6), 16-19.
8. Best, K., & Lewis, J. (2000). Hacking the democratic mainframe: The Melissa virus and transgressive computing. *Media International Australia incorporating Culture and Policy*, 95(1), 207-226.
9. Verini, J. (2010). The great cyberheist. *The New York Times*.

## 4. CYBERCRIME IN THE 21ST CENTURY

1. Olson, P. (2013). *We are anonymous*. Random House.
2. Reilly, M. (2007). Beware, botnets have your PC in their sights.
3. Brenner, S. W., & Schwerha IV, J. J. (2007). Cybercrime Havens Challenges and Solutions. *Bus. L. Today*, 17, 49.
4. https://nakedsecurity.sophos.com/2011/11/24/the-conficker-worm-three-years-and-counting/#:~:targetText=This%20resulted%20in%20many%20more,is%20an%20astoundingly%20large%20figure.
5. Rai, M., & Mandoria, H. L. (2019). A STUDY ON CYBER CRIMES, CYBER CRIMINALS AND MAJOR SECURITY BREACHES.
6. Coleman, G. (2013). Anonymous in context: The politics and power behind the mask.
7. Knuttila, L. (2011). User unknown: 4chan, anonymity and contingency. *First Monday*, 16(10).
8. Pendergrass, S. (2012). Hackers gone wild: the 2011 spring break of lulzsec. *Issues in Information Systems*, 13(1), 133-143.
9. Romagna, M., & van den Hout, N. J. (2017, October). Hacktivism and website defacement: motivations, capabilities and potential threats. In *27th Virus Bulletin International Conference* (Vol. 1).
10. Keall, C. (2019, August). NZ Institute of Directors' website defaced by hacker, passwords at risk. Retrieved from New Zealand Herald: https://www.nzherald.co.nz/business/news/article.cfm?c_id=3&objectid=12255959
11. Nagpal, R. (2008). Evolution of cyber Crimes. *Asian School of Cyber Laws*, 2.
12. Acin, V. (2019). Making sense of the dark web. *Computer Fraud & Security*, 2019(7), 17-19.
13. Caldwell, T. (2011). Ethical hackers: putting on the white hat. *Network Security*, 2011(7), 10-13.

## 5. PHISHING

1. Max Baucus Quotes. (n.d.). BrainyQuote.com. Retrieved October 27, 2019, from BrainyQuote.com Web site: https://www.brainyquote.com/quotes/max_baucus_806619
2. Ferreira, A., & Lenzini, G. (2015, July). An analysis of social engineering principles in effective phishing. In *2015 Workshop on Socio-Technical Aspects in Security and Trust* (pp. 9-16). IEEE.

## 6. BUSINESS EMAIL COMPROMISE

1. Mansfield-Devine, S. (2016). The imitation game: How business email compromise scams are robbing organisations. Computer Fraud & Security, 2016(11), 5-10.

## 7. TECH SUPPORT SCAMS

1. Tabron, J. L. (2016). Creating urgency in tech support scam telephone conversations. Hofstra University.

## 8. OTHER CYBER ENABLED SCAMS

1. Almeshekah, M. H., & Spafford, E. H. (2014, September). Planning and integrating deception into computer security defenses. In Proceedings of the 2014 New Security Paradigms Workshop (pp. 127-138). ACM.
2. Zuckoff, Mitchell. (2005). Annals of crime: The perfect mark. The New Yorker, vol. 82, No. 13, pp. 36-42.
3. Bergiel, B. J., Bergiel, E. B., & Balsmeier, P. W. (2007). I Have a Deal for You: Cross Border Crime. In *Competition Forum* (Vol. 5, No. 1, p. 112). American Society for Competitiveness.

## 9. DDOS AND BOTNETS

1. Mirkovic, J., & Reiher, P. (2004). A taxonomy of DDoS attack and DDoS defense mechanisms. ACM SIGCOMM Computer Communication Review, 34(2), 39-53.
2. https://www.theguardian.com/technology/2012/aug/21/anonymous-hits-government-websites-julian-assange
3. https://www.scmagazineuk.com/article/1483374

4. Mansfield-Devine, S. (2015). The growth and evolution of DDoS. *Network Security*, *2015*(10), 13-20.
5. Upreti, N. (2019). DDoS Attack and Mitigation.
6. Kolias, C., Kambourakis, G., Stavrou, A., & Voas, J. (2017). DDoS in the IoT: Mirai and other botnets. *Computer*, *50*(7), 80-84.
7. Wyke, J. (2011). What is zeus?. *Sophos, May*.
8. Etaher, N., Weir, G. R., & Alazab, M. (2015, August). From zeus to zitmo: Trends in banking malware. In *2015 IEEE Trustcom/BigDataSE/ISPA* (Vol. 1, pp. 1386-1391). IEEE.
9. Zhu, X., Tao, H., Wu, Z., Cao, J., Kalish, K., & Kayne, J. (2017). *Fraud Prevention in Online Digital Advertising*. Springer International Publishing.
10. Mills, R. R. (2018). *The Current State of Insider Threat Awareness and Readiness in Corporate Cyber Security-An Analysis of Definitions, Prevention, Detection and Mitigation* (Doctoral dissertation, Utica College).

## 10. SPYWARE, MALVERTISING AND LOGIC BOMBS

1. Trend Micro. (2019, January). *Spyware Disguises as Android Applications on Google Play*. Retrieved from Trend Micro Blog: https://blog.trendmicro.com/trendlabs-security-intelligence/spyware-disguises-as-android-applications-on-google-play/
2. Shah, S., & Cole, D. (2005). Spyware/adware. In *Proceedings of the Black Hat Conference*.
3. http://pcwhiz.com/stealware-how-stealware-is-used-to-steal-your-revenue/
4. Trend Micro. (2019, January). Spyware Disguises as Android Applications on Google Play. Retrieved from Trend Micro Blog: https://blog.trendmicro.com/trendlabs-security-intelligence/spyware-disguises-as-android-applications-on-google-play/
5. https://blog.malwarebytes.com/cybercrime/2017/05/roughted-the-anti-ad-blocker-malvertiser/
6. Siemens Contract Employee Intentionally Damaged Computers by Planting Logic Bombs into Programs He Designed". www.justice.gov. United States Department of Justice. 19 July 2019
7. https://www.zdnet.com/article/siemens-contractor-pleads-guilty-to-planting-logic-bomb-in-company-spreadsheets/

## 11. TROJANS, KEY LOGGERS AND CRYPTOJACKING

1. Musch, M., Wressnegger, C., Johns, M., & Rieck, K. (2018). Web-based Cryptojacking in the Wild. arXiv preprint arXiv:1808.09474.
2. Wei, C., Sprague, A., & Warner, G. (2008, March). Detection of networks blocks used by the Storm Worm botnet. In *Proceedings of the 46th Annual Southeast Regional Conference on XX* (pp. 356-360). ACM.
3. Jedynak, J., & Kotowicz, M. Peering into spam botnets.

## 12. RANSOMWARE

1. Brewer, R. (2016). Ransomware attacks: detection, prevention and cure. Network Security, 2016(9), 5-9.
2. Mohurle, S., & Patil, M. (2017). A brief study of wannacry threat: Ransomware attack 2017. *International Journal of Advanced Research in Computer Science*, 8(5).
3. Malwarebytes (n.d.). GandCrab Retrieved November 12, 2019, from Malwarebytes.com Web site: https://www.malwarebytes.com/gandcrab/
4. Davis, J. (2018). SamSam ransomware hackers bank $8 million and counting from victims. Retrieved 18 November 2019, from https://www.healthcareit.com.au/article/samsam-ransomware-hackers-bank-8-million-and-counting-victims
5. Kearney, L. (2018). Atlanta ransomware attack throws city services into disarray
6. Kearney, L. (2018). Atlanta officials reveal worsening effects of cyber attack. Retrieved 18 November 2019, from https://www.reuters.com/article/us-usa-cyber-atlanta-budget/atlanta-officials-reveal-worsening-effects-of-cyber-attack-idUSKCN1J231M?feedType=RSS&feedName=technologyNews
7. Dean, A. T. (2019). *The Growth of Ransomware and Its Impact on City Governments* (Doctoral dissertation, Utica College).
8. Kajiloti, M. (2019). PureLocker: New Ransomware-as-a-Service Being Used in Targeted Attacks Against Servers. Retrieved from Intezer: https://www.intezer.com/blog-purelocker-ransomware-being-used-in-targeted-attacks-against-servers/
9. https://www.zdnet.com/article/company-shuts-down-because-of-ransomware-leaves-300-without-jobs-just-before-holidays/

## 13. CYBERCRIME - BULLYING AND EXPLOITATION

1. Campbell, M. A. (2005). Cyber bullying: An old problem in a new guise?. *Journal of Psychologists and Counsellors in Schools, 15*(1), 68-76.
2. Goodno, N. H. (2007). Cyberstalking, a new crime: Evaluating the effectiveness of current state and federal laws. *Mo. L. Rev., 72*, 125.
3. https://www.unicef.org/press-releases/unicef-poll-more-third-young-people-30-countries-report-being-victim-online-bullying

## 14. DATA BREACHES AND PRIVACY

1. Gatzlaff, K. M., & McCullough, K. A. (2010). The effect of data breaches on shareholder wealth. *Risk Management and Insurance Review, 13*(1), 61-83.
2. Tehan, R., & Knowledge Services Group. (2005, December). Personal data security breaches: Context and incident summaries. Congressional Research Service, Library of Congress.
3. Acquisti, A., Friedman, A., & Telang, R. (2006). Is there a cost to privacy breaches? An event study. *ICIS 2006 Proceedings*, 94.

## 15. CYBERCRIME - THE PERPETRATORS

1. Tropina, T. (2010). Cybercrime and organized crime. *Freedom from Fear, 2010*(7), 16-17.
2. Richards, J. R. (1998). *Transnational criminal organizations, cybercrime, and money laundering: a handbook for law enforcement officers, auditors, and financial investigators.* CRC press.
3. Nurse, J. R., & Bada, M. (2019). The group element of cybercrime: Types, dynamics, and criminal operations. *arXiv preprint arXiv:1901.01914.*
4. Bayoumy, Y. (2018). *Cybercrime Economy-A Netnographic Study on the Dark Net Ecosystem for Ransomware* (Master's thesis, NTNU).
5. Geers, K., Kindlund, D., Moran, N., & Rachwald, R. (2014). World War C: Understanding nation-state motives behind today's advanced cyber attacks. *FireEye Inc., Milpitas, CA.*
6. Workman, M., Phelps, D. C., & Hare, R. C. (2013). A study of performative hactivist subcultures and threats to businesses. *Information Security Journal: A Global Perspective, 22*(4), 187-200.
7. Ludlow, P. (2010). Wikileaks and hacktivist culture. *The Nation, 4*, 25-26.

## 16. CYBERCRIME - CHALLENGES FOR LAW ENFORCEMENT

1. Ng, J. (2016). International cybercrime, transnational evidence gathering and the challenges in Australia: finding the delicate balance. *International Journal of Information and Communication Technology*, 9(2), 177-198.
2. Grabosky, P., (2004) The Global Dimension of Cybercrime, Global Crime, 6:1, 146-157, DOI: 10.1080/1744057042000297034
3. Harkin, D., Whelan, C., & Chang, L. (2018). The challenges facing specialist police cyber-crime units: an empirical analysis. *Police Practice and Research*, 19(6), 519-536.
4. Nouh, M., Nurse, J. R., Webb, H., & Goldsmith, M. (2019). Cybercrime Investigators are Users Too! Understanding the Socio-Technical Challenges Faced by Law Enforcement. *arXiv preprint arXiv:1902.06961*.
5. Dolliver, D. S. (2019). Emerging Technologies, Law Enforcement Responses, and National Security. *ISJLP*, 15, 123.
6. Leukfeldt, E. R., Notté, R. J., & Malsch, M. (2020). Exploring the Needs of Victims of Cyber-dependent and Cyber-enabled Crimes. *Victims & Offenders*, 15(1), 60-77.

## 17. WHAT IS CYBERSECURITY?

1. Da Veiga, A. (2016, July). A cybersecurity culture research philosophy and approach to develop a valid and reliable measuring instrument. In *2016 SAI Computing Conference (SAI)* (pp. 1006-1015). IEEE.

## 18. TECHNOLOGY FOR CYBERSECURITY

1. Toth, P., & Klein, P. (2013). A role-based model for federal information technology/cyber security training. *NIST special publication*, 800(16), 1-152.

## 19. CYBERSECURITY - VULNERABILITIES

1. Choo, K. K. R. (2011). The cyber threat landscape: Challenges and future research directions. Computers & Security, 30(8), 719-731.
2. https://cve.mitre.org/about/index.html#cve_community
3. Greenberg, Andy (2019-11-02). "The First BlueKeep Mass Hacking

Is Finally Here—but Don't Panic - After months of warnings, the first successful attack using Microsoft's BlueKeep vulnerability has arrived—but isn't nearly as bad as it could have been". Wired.
4. Carlin, D., Burgess, J., O'Kane, P., & Sezer, S. (2019). You could be mine (d): the rise of cryptojacking. *IEEE Security & Privacy*.
5. Minkin, M., Moghimi, D., Lipp, M., Schwarz, M., Van Bulck, J., Genkin, D., ... & Yarom, Y. (2019). Fallout: Reading Kernel Writes From User Space. *arXiv preprint arXiv:1905.12701*.
6. Kocher, P., Horn, J., Fogh, A., Genkin, D., Gruss, D., Haas, W., ... & Schwarz, M. (2019, May). Spectre attacks: Exploiting speculative execution. In *2019 IEEE Symposium on Security and Privacy (SP)* (pp. 1-19). IEEE.
7. Alhubaiti, O., & El-Alfy, E. S. M. (2019, September). Impact of Spectre/Meltdown Kernel Patches on Crypto-Algorithms on Windows Platforms. In *2019 International Conference on Innovation and Intelligence for Informatics, Computing, and Technologies (3ICT)* (pp. 1-6). IEEE.

## 20. CAREERS IN CYBER SECURITY

1. Csorny, L. (2013). Careers in the growing field of information technology services.
2. Fitzgerald, T. (2018). *CISO COMPASS: Navigating Cybersecurity Leadership Challenges with Insights from Pioneers*. Auerbach Publications.
3. Murphy, C. N., & Yates, J. (2009). *The International Organization for Standardization (ISO): global governance through voluntary consensus*. Routledge.
4. Barafort, B., Mesquida, A. L., & Mas, A. (2017). Integrating risk management in IT settings from ISO standards and management systems perspectives. *Computer Standards & Interfaces*, 54, 176-185.
5. Sinha, S. (2019). Injecting Unintended XML. In *Bug Bounty Hunting for Web Security* (pp. 123-146). Apress, Berkeley, CA.

## 21. A BRIEF HISTORY OF COMPUTERS

1. Misa, T. J. (2016). Charles Babbage, Ada Lovelace, and the Bernoulli numbers. In Ada's Legacy: Cultures of Computing from the Victorian to the Digital Age (pp. 11-31). Association for Computing Machinery.
2. Hughes, C., & Hughes, T. (2019). The laws of thought and thinking machines. *AI Matters*, 5(1), 20-24.
3. http://www.fourmilab.ch/babbage/sketch.html

4. Hoffmann, D. W. (2010). *Grundlagen der technischen Informatik* (Vol. 5). Hanser.
5. Rojas, R. (1997). Konrad Zuse's legacy: the architecture of the Z1 and Z3. *IEEE Annals of the History of Computing, 19*(2), 5-16.
6. Phillips, A. (1982). Project Whirlwind: The History of A Pioneer Computer. By Kent C. Redmond and Thomas M. Smith. Bedford, Mass., Digital Press, 1980. Pp. xiv+ 280. $21.00.-Early Rritish Computers. By Simon Lavington. Bedford, Mass., Digital Press, 1980. Pp. 139. $8.00. *Business History Review, 56*(3), 461-463.
7. Ward, S. (1998). Taken for granted. *Physics World, 11*(2), 22.
8. Todd, K. D. (2015). Jean Jennings Bartik: Computer Pioneer. Truman State University Press.
9. Blackburn, R. (2017). The secret life of Hedy Lamarr.
10. Ross, H. D. (1953). The arithmetic element of the IBM type 701 computer. *Proceedings of the IRE, 41*(10), 1287-1294.
11. Hutchins, W. J. (2004, September). The Georgetown-IBM experiment demonstrated in January 1954. In *Conference of the Association for Machine Translation in the Americas* (pp. 102-114). Springer, Berlin, Heidelberg.
12. Zannos, S. (2002). *Edward Roberts and the Story of the Personal Computer*. Mitchell Lane Pub Incorporated.
13. Martens, B., & Wiser, B. (2013). *The Wozpak Special Edition: Steve Wozniak's Apple-1 & Apple][Computers*. Lulu. com.
14. Carlton, J., & Annotations-Kawasaki, G. (1997). *Apple: The inside story of intrigue, egomania, and business blunders*. Random House Inc..

## 22. THE WORLD OF THE WEB

1. ilva, D. (2009, April 22). *Internet has only just begun, say founders*. Retrieved from Phys Org: https://phys.org/news/2009-04-Internet-begun-founders.html
2. Leiner, B. M., Cerf, V. G., Clark, D. D., Kahn, R. E., Kleinrock, L., Lynch, D. C., ... & Wolff, S. S. (1997). The past and future history of the Internet. *Communications of the ACM, 40*(2), 102-108.
3. Friedman, L. W., & Friedman, H. H. (2015). Connectivity and convergence: A whimsical history of Internet culture. *Available at SSRN 2628901*.
4. Press, L. (1986). The ACM conference on the history of personal workstations. *ACM SIGSMALL/PC Notes, 12*(4), 3-10.
5. Villalva, D. A. B., Onaolapo, J., Stringhini, G., & Musolesi, M. (2018). Under and over the surface: a comparison of the use of leaked account credentials in the Dark and Surface Web. *Crime Science, 7*(1), 17.
6. https://www.torproject.org/about/history/
7. Dredge, S. (2013). What is Tor? A beginner's guide to the privacy

tool. The Guardian, 5.
8. Kalberg, Å. H. (2017). *An Endeavour in the Domain of Cybercrime: Exploring the Structural and Cultural Features of the Darknet Market AlphaBay* (Master's thesis).

## 23. PROTECTION FROM CYBERCRIME

1. Stephensen, N. (2019, August). Retrieved from Linked In: https://www.linkedin.com/posts/nicole-stephensen-privacymatters_the-easier-we-make-it-for-ourselves-the-activity-6570493972702203904-sdJ_
2. Cross, C. (2015). No laughing matter: Blaming the victim of online fraud. *International Review of Victimology*, 21(2), 187-204.

## 24. UNMASKING THE HACKER

1. Mitch Kapor Quotes. (n.d.). BrainyQuote.com. Retrieved October 27, 2019, from BrainyQuote.com Web site: https://www.brainyquote.com/quotes/mitch_kapor_690457

# GLOSSARY

**4CHAN**
An online forum where users can post images and create discussions anonymously

**Antivirus**
Application designed to detect and remove malware

**APT**
Advanced persistent threat - a prolonged and targeted cybercrime campaign where criminals gain access to restricted networks or computers and remains undetected for a time

**Ark**
A computer at the Digital Equipment Corporation

**ARPANET**
Advanced Research Projects Agency Network, precursor to the internet

## Backdoor
A way to bypass security measures to gain access to a network

## Black listing
Firewall configuration that by default allows all traffic through and blocks only known malicious entities

## Botnets
Network of computers infected by malware and acting together

## Browser
An application used to access the internet

## Business Email Compromise
Type of email scam mimicking employees or businesses to obtain money or information

## CCTV
Closed-Circuit television, a type of video surveillance

## CERT
Computer (or Cyber) Emergency Response (or Readiness) Team

## CISO
Chief Information Security Officer, responsible for overseeing the cyber and information security strategies and policies of an organisation

## Cryptojacking
Uses a computer to mine crypto currency without the user's knowledge or authorisation and can slow down the
impacted devices.

## CVE
Common Vulnerabilities and Exposures is a public domain register of discovered application vulnerabilities

## Dark Net
Non-indexed part of the internet requiring a special browser to access

## DDoS
Distributed Denial of Service - malicious disruption of network traffic with multiple computers

## Deep Net
Non-indexed part of the internet

## DNS
Domain Name Server - translates domain names into numbers, called IP Addresses, so computers can understand them

## DNS tunnelling
Exploiting the protocol to transfer malware and data to a victim's network or computer

**DoS**
Denial of Service - malicious disruption of network traffic with one computer

**Drive by download**
Malware automatically downloaded to a computer

**Email client**
An application to receive, send, read and write emails

**ENIAC**
Electronic Numerical Integrator and Computer

**Firewall**
Hardware or software application that filters internet traffic

**Internet**
Global network infrastructure in which the World Wide Web sits

**IoT**
Internet of Things - internet connected devices and things

**IP address**
Internet Protocol that identifies computers using the Internet to communicate.

**IRC**
Internet Relay Chat

## ISO
International Organization for Standardization is an independent International body founded in 1946 that aims to bring consistency to products and services by publishing framework and guidelines documents

## Keylogger
Software or hardware that records the keystrokes of a user without their knowledge

## Logic Bomb
Code secretly embedded in an application that will execute once a particular condition is met

## MaaS
Malware as a service

## Malvertising
Malicious code embedded in legitimate advertisements or in spoofed advertisements on web sites

## Malware
Malicious software

## Malware signatures
Malware signatures are the unique values that the malicious programmes have, like a fingerprint for code

## Morris Worm
Self replicating malware created by Robert Morris and released in 1988

**Multi-factor authentication**
Is a way to verify a user's authority to access a network or account by providing different credentials such as something you know (eg a password), something you have (eg a PIN from a token) and something you are (such as fingerprint).

**Patch**
Software update or change to a system or application

**Payload**
Malware that is sent to a computer or other smart Internet connected device, downloaded and installed without the user's knowledge.

**Pen testing**
Penetration testing tests networks, computers and processes for vulnerabilities that may be exploited

**Phishing**
Emails spoofing known companies to trick recipients into providing information or downloading malware

**PIN**
Personal identification number

**Punch card**
A card that has perforations in it representing computer code

## GLOSSARY

**Ransomware**
Malware that locks computers or encrypts files demanding a ransom be paid in exchange for unlocking or decrypting

**Remote Access Trojan (RAT)**
Malware that gives a criminal administrative access of the victim's computer

**Rootkit**
Malware used to gain access to a computer or restricted systems

**Social Engineering**
Psychological manipulation of people used to trick them

**Spam**
Unsolicited bulk email

**Spam filter**
Technology that uses a set of rules to work out whether an email is malicious

**Spoofed email address**
Email address designed to appear as if from a trusted source

**Spyware**
Malware that spies on the users' network activity and data without their knowledge

## TOR
The Onion Router - A free and open-source browser that provides anonymous internet communication

## Traffic
Data transmitted to or from a network

## Trojan
Malware that appears to be benign software

## URL
Uniform Resource Locator - a web address

## USB
Universal Serial Bus is a type of connection for power, peripheral devices or flash drives

## Virus
Self-replicating malware that requires a user to first run

## Vishing
Phone calls spoofing known companies to trick recipients into providing information

## VPN
Virtual Private Network is a tool that allows a user to browse the internet anonymously and encrypting the network traffic

## Web defacement
Pages of a compromised website are replaced with an image or message

**White listing**
Firewall configuration that by default blocks all traffic and allows only known trusted entities

**Worm**
Stand alone self-replicating malware

**Y2K bug**
A potential bug due to how years were recorded in code that may have caused issues when computers went from 1999 to 2000

**Zero-Day Vulnerability**
A computer or network vulnerability that is not known or not mitigated and can be exploited

# INDEX

**4Chan** 26

**Ada Lovelace** 144

**Anonymous** 23, 26

**AOHell** 18

**AOL** 17, 18, 19

**Ark** 11, 12

**ARPANET** 12, 149

**Babbage** 4, 143-145

**Black listing** 128, 129

**Blue box** 10

**Captain Crunch** *see John Draper*

**Colossus** 145

**Conficker worm** 25

**Cryptojacking** 91, 96

**CVE** 132

**Data breach** 60, 109-112

**DDoS** 25, 69-77

**Emotet** 89, 90

**Engressia** 9, 10

**ENIAC** 145-147

**Firewall** 124, 129

**Gameover Zeus** 75

**ILOVEYOU worm** 25

**iSKORPITX** 28

**John Calce** *see Mafia Boy*

**John Draper** 10, 11

**Jonathan James** 20

**Joy Bubbles** *see Engressia*

**Kevin Mitnick** 11, 12, 18, 21

**Kevin Poulsen** 12

**Lizard Squad** 73

**Logic Bomb** 79, 83, 84

**LulzSec** 27

**Mafia Boy** 26

**Marconi** 5, 6, 155

**Melissa virus** 19, 20

**MethBot** 74

**Mirai** 74

**MobSTSPY** 82

**Phantom Squad** 73

**Phone Phreak** 9-12

**Phonemasters** 16, 18, 21

**Punch card** 4, 6, 136, 137

**Ralph Barclay** 10

**Solar sunrise** 19

**Steve Jobs** 10, 146

**Steve Wozniak** 10, 146

**WannaCry** 97

**Whistler** *see Engressia*

**White listing** 129

**Y2K** 16, 17

**Zero-day** 132

**Zeus** 74, 75

# ABOUT THE DEMYSTIFY CYBER PROJECT

Project mission: to demystify cyber to support everyone to be safer online and when using technology.

This book is part of my initiative, Demystify Cyber, to help users of technology to better understand cyber security and stay safer from cybercrime. The concept for this first came about in 2018 when I was lecturing a group of criminology students. What I thought everyone knew, about online safety and cybercrime, was not as common knowledge as I had presumed. Realising that increased interconnectivity and other advances in technology will also lead to an increase in crime opportunities, I was concerned that so many users of technology do not have the basic knowledge they need to keep themselves safe online.

. . .

Thank you for your interest in supporting a more cyber safe community.

# ABOUT THE AUTHOR

*Amanda-Jane was in the first cohort to be named a Fellow of the Australian Information Security Association (AISA) in 2019 and has won multiple infosec industry awards. She is a firm believer that diversity in all its forms should be encouraged to promote innovation and find solutions to challenges facing the world. She currently works at the University of Queensland (UQ) as the manager of the Cyber Security Operations Centre. Prior to that she worked as a Senior Cyber Crime Intelligence Analyst with the Australian Government. She has held various roles including security incident response, malware analysis, digital forensics, communications, and fraud investigator. She volunteers at AISA as the Brisbane Branch Executive Chair, is the co-founder and Australian Director of Cyber Century Mentoring, a Justice of the Peace and, an Adjunct Lecturer in Criminology at UQ. From 2016 to 2018 she supported the Australian Women in Security Network (AWSN) by coding, creating and promoting their first blog and was an interim chapter lead in Queensland. Amanda-Jane mentors students and those new to the infosec industry, speaks at conferences and has guest lectured at Griffith University. She writes about cybercrime and security, tweets as @empressbat, plays MMORPG and her drink of choice is coffee.*

www.ingramcontent.com/pod-product-compliance
Lightning Source LLC
Chambersburg PA
CBHW070626220526
45466CB00001B/106